"A.J. Swoboda reveals a Bible chock-full of lives filled with God's presence but fraught with blunder, betrayal, and frustration. All human beings are a mess and prone to mess things up. But in the midst of all this messiness, which the author details with humor and charm, Swoboda shows how a Divine Messenger breaks through with messages of hope, massages of beauty, and safe passages of peace."
—LEONARD SWEET, best-selling author, professor at Drew University and George Fox University, and chief contributor to sermons.com

"A.J. Swoboda made me laugh so hard I forgot we were talking about the Bible. I want to say this book is a 'breath of fresh air' but it's more than that: this book is a reminder to breathe. Every chapter is another glorious gulp of pure oxygen."
—MATT MIKALATOS, author of *My Imaginary Jesus* and *Night of the Living Dead Christian*

"Swoboda describes what we rarely discuss—that the journey of becoming a Christlike community, a church, is not a pretty line from A to Z but a dizzying mess of contradictions and struggles. Through story, humor, and biblical and theological insights, Swoboda gives us a refreshing picture of hope for the church as a real place for real people who want to love and live like Jesus. Fun and provocative, this book is a must-read for any Christian who wonders about the church today."
—MARYKATE MORSE, author of *Making Room for Leadership*

"The reality is, we all live messy lives cluttered with disarray and mayhem. As Jesus followers, we desperately need a major revision of how we see ourselves from God's perspective. A.J. Swoboda brilliantly portrays the picture of God wading deep into the mess of our reality, eager to embrace us fully. Through each chapter, A.J. gives us a fresh and profound insight that will stimulate and ignite our relationship with God. You will find *Messy: God Likes It That Way* inspiring, compelling, authentic, and funny."

—MIKE TATLOCK, lead pastor of Grace Chapel and author of *Faith in Real Life*

"A.J. has a way with words. He's a master at taking ancient, well-known truths and wrapping them up in fresh, creative language that captures the mind and the soul. At a time when young people are leaving the church in droves, *Messy: God Likes It That Way* comes as a glimmer of hope on the horizon. It's a must-read for anybody who wants to recapture the beauty of Jesus and his messy church."

—JOHN MARK COMER, pastor of Solid Rock Church, Portland, OR

MESSY

MESSY

God Likes It That Way

A.J. SWOBODA

Kregel
Publications

Messy: God Likes It That Way
© 2012 by A.J. Swoboda

Published by Kregel Publications, a division of Kregel, Inc., P.O. Box 2607, Grand Rapids, MI 49501.

Library of Congress Cataloging-in-Publication Data

ISBN 978-0-8254-4168-4

Printed in the United States of America

12 13 14 15 16 / 5 4 3 2

For Quinn.
'Til glory hands we'll hold.

CONTENTS

ACKNOWLEDGMENTS

You never really finish a book, you just stop writing it.

This book breathes and many people have blown into its nostrils to give it life. Some of them I want to briefly acknowledge.

My best friend and wife, Quinn; thanks for the pad thai and ¿Por Qué No? throughout the birthing of this book. Speaking of birthing . . . To the child that came out of you: Elliot, I love you, little buddy. You're an alien but we'll keep you. This is my family.

My parents were nice enough to make me. Thank you endlessly. I *literally* couldn't have done this without you.

Nate. If you hadn't gone to Taco Bell with me, who knows where I'd be. Steve, George, and Jim; my Three Amigos. Thanks for helping me face my *El Guapos* around every corner. Dr. Dan Brunner, Dr. Mark Cartledge, and Dr. MaryKate Morse have been friends and supporters every step of the way. Randy, Kip, Ann, and Jared all let me preach in the pulpit and had to answer e-mails because of it. For that I am grateful and sorry.

My friend Laurel, upon first reading this book, stared at me blankly. Then she said she could work with it. Thanks for initial edits; you're incredible.

Acknowledgments

Kregel Publications. If I wanted, I could have taken my talents to South Beach. I just happen to like Grand Rapids more. Thanks for believing in me. Steve Barclift and Cat Hoort have been great yolkfellows along the way. Paul Brinkerhoff is too smart for any business. Thanks for reading my stuff anyway. Also, David Van Diest is a great agent. Hire him if you need one.

Steve Jobs. You died this year and we're all super sad. Thanks for all the stuff you invented. I wrote my book using some of it.

Jeannie St. John Taylor. You might write children's books, but you inspire us all. Thanks for the gracious love and support with the occasional meal to encourage. I owe you one.

Theophilus. Please remember me when you're famous.

The Trinity of the Father, the Son, and the Spirit. Thanks for speaking us all into life and then sovereignly letting us invent computers to write stuff about you for other people to read. You are life. You are hope. And I'm in awe.

INTRODUCTION

My rickety old house has this little room full of cleaning supplies, brooms, bleach, and little yellow gloves. This room has never been organized. It's our cleaning room and it's always messy. Every once in a long while, I take a Saturday to clean up our house: dusting, vacuuming, arranging DVDs, scrubbing the little metal cup that holds my toothbrush. It's a momentous affair. And it always takes me back to that little messy cleaning room.

The messiest room in my house is the one full of things that make it beautiful.

That's what Christian faith is like. It's a thing that gives beauty and meaning and purpose to life yet it's still messy like that little cleaning room.

Here's to finding God in that mess.

CHAPTER ONE

A Bush That Shakes: The Mess

In ancient Greek and Latin theatre, there would often be a character representing the gods. This character's name was the Deus ex Machina. It means "God of the machine." It was a character who had an exceptionally important role in the plot of the story. At the moment in the play when everything seemed at its worst, when all problems seemed beyond control or resolve, when the main character is about to be killed by the villain and everything is beyond fixability, this character would come out on stage. This was Deus ex Machina: the machine-god. And at just the right moment, the machine-god would swoop on stage, wave his magic wand over the whole messy thing, and the mess would be fixed. *Kazam. Whammo.* Finis. Curtain. Play over. Happy ending. Pay the babysitter.

We could use one of those gods right about now, couldn't we? It sounds like the very thing we need to fix this whole mess we seem to have gotten ourselves into. But we may be in for a long wait. And we probably shouldn't quit the day job.

Because that god only does theatre.

It Is What It Is

I once heard a guy say that Santa is the ultimate hipster; he works one day a year and spends the rest of it judging you. Jesus is like that for a lot of people. And they're finding out it doesn't work.

Christianity is surprisingly messier than what I signed up for. I'm sure many of us would admit that. A famous pastor's kid once said near the end of his life that he'd have become a Christian if he'd ever actually met one. His problem was, the only one he'd ever heard of apparently died on a cross.[1] He saw the mess. And ran. Few of us admittingly accept it, but it's true. This whole thing is just one big mess, isn't it? Preaching a beautiful message of grace, we so rarely, if ever, practice it on each other. Let alone ourselves. Christians not acting like Christians. Churches not being the thing we think church should be. People renouncing God because of the hypocrisy of the people who follow him. Churches splitting like multicell amoeba. So on and so forth. You have to admit—most of the time, it all feels like one big fat mess.

Look, I get it. Really. And of course, not helping is the minor detail that God sometimes seems oddly quiet about the whole thing. We all secretly wish God would fix it all up with one fell swoop by some magical moment with divine lightning. *Kazam. Whammo.* It's understandable to me why some continue to predict this soon-coming apocalyptic catastrophe that'll apparently magically fix everything.

---

1. The kid's name was Friedrich Nietzsche. Oddly enough, sadly, in the history of the world, pastors' kids (PKs) are notorious for becoming atheists, existentialist nihilists, and the like.

They describe a really angry God who descends in all his divine cruelness to fix it all by judging nonbelievers and pagans and liberals with storms and earthquakes and gnats. And then, just *then*, it will all return to the way it's supposed to be. Problem fixed. But for those who watch the news, there has yet to be such a resolve, for we're still here. And so are the nonbelievers, the pagans, and the liberals.

And me too.

This is somewhat problematic. For a God of order that the Bible appears to describe, there seems to be a lot of messiness in the world. So either God is hopelessly out of control, or God, in all God's God-ness, fancies himself content with letting us, the human race, run around invariably being human, making fools of ourselves. And this because the point isn't about everything here on earth being fixed. It's about something else. Something that we don't want to hear.

About how important the mess is to being authentically human.

Mind you, it's not just Christianity that's got a mess on its religious hands. No doubt, Christianity from page one has been surprisingly messy. But you have been too. So have the Muslims and the Green Party and ToysRUs. It's all messy. Christian or not. Religious or not. It's not like Christianity is all screwed up but we're walking around with halos on our head. We as humans are the messed up ones. Sometimes I sit up late at night and wonder why I'm so messed up. Why I can't change myself. Why there's not some Rosetta Stone CD set that can fix me and teach me how to be better in four easy installments.

Sometimes we lose hope. We feel so alone. And in our weaker moments, we secretly judge those who appear on the outside to have it all together. This isn't a book for them. Because *their* story has never been *my* story. Nor has it been yours. Your story is messy like mine. There are lots of books that sell by falsely encouraging you, the reader, to flee church, community, and God altogether. They say to flee the faith. Flee Christianity. Flee it all. Flee the mess. Become your own person. You don't need those crutches anymore. And those books are right about one thing. *The mess.* But what's so surprising is how those who have left God, left the faith, left community, *are still screwed up.* They're just screwed up without God, without faith, without community. What they're disgustingly wrong about is how central the mess is to being a human. And how the mess is necessary.

And how it is what it is.

The Flying-Monkey God

I met God in math class. It was during second period, spring sophomore geometry in high school. I hate math but that's where I met God, so math is always going to be part of my story. God's a comedian like that.

Some people tell their story about meeting God miraculously when they were coming off a crack high or had just finished stripping or something like that. And those are beautiful, incredible stories. I wish mine was more like that. Mine was ten minutes before lunch in Homeroom 221B. To this day it remains a very mysterious memory to me. I remember sitting in math next to my friend Robert and these two girls for a group project on the Pythagorean theorem. These two girls started talking with Robert about God, Jesus, and the end of the world. They started arguing about this book I'd never heard about from something called the Left Behind series. It was this enigmatic story about how a really ticked-off Jesus was soon coming back and appeared to be really perturbed at everyone and how the president of some European country turns out to be Satan with horns and stuff, and people that didn't like Jesus were in a real heap of trouble if they didn't submit. Apparently those who liked Jesus would be fine. So I just sat there, glibly considering my eternal situation that put me a little south of paradise. But I listened. Not minding my own business. That was my introduction to God. The God they spoke of sounded mean. And bent on destruction. Like the witch from Oz. The bad one. With the flying monkeys.

Something unexpected happened inside of me. Something awoke, like a monster that came to his senses deep down in the crevices of my soul. So I did what I saw Christians do in movies and coffee shops; I went home and opened my Bible. That's all I knew what to do. I clamored through some dusty boxes and found the only Bible I could. It was this King James Version with all of the untos and thous that my old man gave me from when he was in college. I thought for something holy, it was surprisingly dusty. Sitting there in my room I just stared at it, waiting to see what would happen. Silently. Not knowing what to do with it, I did that thing where you just open up wherever it opens up and half-jokingly whisper to heaven, "Okay, God of the universe, I'm going to open up your Bible wherever I opened it and you will speak to me out of the randomness of chance." I opened my Bible and started reading from this section at the beginning. It was called Leviticus. It was filled with blood and sacrifice and Moses making lots of rules; I was pretty sure it sounded like a handbook for a cult.

Setting it on the green carpet of my bedroom floor, I almost gave up. But then I gave it a second chance. Flipping it open again, I read the stuff to the right, where the words were different colors, some in red. I started in this book named after a guy called Matthew; it had stories about these two brothers who started to follow this Jesus, and finally I thought, *These are intriguing stories.*

This Jesus fellow was so mysterious and beautiful to me. No question. What I was struck by was how the people who followed Jesus were low-level chumps. It was wonderfully disturbing that Jesus associated himself with losers, because it would make sense that he would hang out with someone like me. And even more than that, Jesus called the chumps and changed the world with them. *Jesus and the chumps.* Sounded like my kind of club. Jesus said to the chumps, "Come and follow me." And the chumps did.

That phrase rang in my heart all night long. "Follow me."

A week later, driving to the YMCA to play basketball downtown,

I became a Christian in my car. I wasn't listening to K-LOVE or anything. It was just simple. Those words wouldn't go away. Like a ringing in my ear; a humming that wouldn't end. *Come. Follow. Me.* In my red Mazda pickup, at sixteen years old, driving downtown to play basketball at the YMCA, I gave my heart and soul to what I thought was this voice in my head with all I had and all I was and all I would be. It just happened. I wept in my car. All alone. Alive. I'm convinced to this day that this was the only time in history that God has ever worked in a math class. I'm also the only person I know who accidentally became a Christian by not minding his own business in math class.

God was so new to me. A girlfriend at the time told me that Jesus wanted me to go to church. So I went. After asking around, a friend told me about this little Baptist place with a youth group. This was where I met Christianity. For me, Christianity was weirder than Jesus. But good at the same time. In Christianity, I found, there were lots of cute girls. They were weird though. They wanted to pray and read the Bible with me, which was slightly different than my agenda. I dated one of them. She was very helpful. She told me about God and the Bible and that I couldn't have sex with her. Again, *very* helpful. We all need boundaries. After a year or so, I began to make some important changes in my life. Some of the stupid things sixteen-year-old boys do, I learned, weren't the most valued in the Christian tradition. I tried with all my might to stop those things because it seemed they made Jesus mad. Soon, the church became my family. I brought my mom to church and she became a Christian. It was all so exciting.

Mess

Ten years later, things have changed. I've started hearing things that I didn't hear in years past. In private conversations behind closed doors when no one is looking. Over coffee. At dinner. On the phone at 11 PM. There's this one thing that keeps coming up that no one really wants to talk about on Sunday; like a dirty little secret. It's about Christianity, faith, God, the Bible. You name it. All these things. How all these things are way more messy than we put on. How we don't have them all figured out like we think we should. And there's a reason why we don't talk about this stuff in public. It makes us look bad. It makes us look like we're a joke. It makes us look like we don't know what we are doing. But we're secretly talking about this stuff. Just, *quietly*. It's like there's this secret club within Christianity of people who have given up on the idea that Christianity, or faith, or the church are these perfect pristine things that will save the world. So we have quiet conversations amongst ourselves when no one else is listening and the microphone is off. In dark corners. In coffee shops. Behind closed doors. So no one gets in trouble. So no one thinks we're traitors. But ultimately, if the club got together, lots of us would probably be there.

The club has figured out that Christianity far underperforms the Christ it talks about.

It's not like those in the club have given up. Not at all. There are things that we can't get away from. Things we can't escape. Jesus, as God in the flesh, is unbelievably beautiful and saves us from everything about ourselves. Check. God is majestic and still makes room for morons. Check. The Holy Spirit is real and makes life so much more exciting and real. Check. No doubts about any of these things. It's just the marketing systems around Jesus that we've built, our broken religious systems, our attempts to understand God in logical and compartmentalized ways—*are all inherently flawed and imperfect*. Our faith is much more messy, more gray, than we like to put on. We're messed up. We've all attempted to fix ourselves in one way or another, only to fail time and time again. We've tried to make church look so good on the outside that everyone thinks we've made it and have it all together. It becomes Chia church. Hollow and empty with a glossy look of life on the outside without the sprouts on the outside. And for lots of us, it just isn't working.

After trying, we go home and realize what we've done—like we're waking up from a dream. Even if it did seem to work under a thin veneer of deception, the real us knew it was fake. Deep down, the real us groaned for freedom. We in the club know the feeling. We have unending questions about God, faith, church, you name it. The list goes on because there's no limit to the mess. Others of us are in a mess of unanswered prayers, of painful choices, of regrets unresolved, of faith falling apart at the very seams. Sadly, no quick fix has been found. Like fingerprints, every messy life is different. We catch ourselves thinking about the mess in the shower. We just can't seem to get it all right. But what if the mess is holy? What if the mess is the way it's all supposed to be? What if the mess is not something to "fix"? Just look at how God made the world.

Because God invents the mess.

Bereshit

Bereshit. This is the Bible's opening word. Loosely, it means "in the beginning." Mind you, it's pronounced "bara-*sheet.*" I discovered that the hard way early on a Thursday morning in a class on biblical Hebrew at the seminary I went to. Sitting in a circle, we slowly read the Old Testament out loud in Hebrew, and I quickly learned that a slight variance in the pronunciation of the first word in the biblical narrative, and the Bible's introduction takes on a somewhat darker, PG-13 undertone. Maybe even R. *Bereshit bara Elohim 'et hashamayim v'et ha'aretz.* That's the Bible's entire first sentence. It translates roughly into, "In the beginning God created the heavens and the earth." This is an important point of the story. Now like most music, you can tell a lot about the rest of the album from the first couple of songs.

There is some interesting stuff in sentence numero uno. For instance, the first name used for God in the Bible is *Elohim.*[2] It has a couple

---

2. Much of this material has been inspired by the classic *From Creation to the Cross: Understanding the First Half of the Bible* by Albert H. Baylis (Zondervan, 1996), first published as *On the Way to Jesus* (Multnomah, 1986).

of meanings; *Elohim* can simply mean "god" or in Hebrew the word *Elohim* is often plural and can mean "gods." Smart Bible people tell us this can have a number of interpretations. First, it can mean that God is in some sense, even from the beginning of the Bible, one and many. It's interesting because later on God comments that he will make Adam and Eve in "our" image. That is, *Elohim* (God and gods) speaks to the fact that God is one and many. Sure, you could say that's the Trinity, which is fine. But it is unlikely the writers of the Old Testament had that in mind. Yet it is one interpretation. It can also mean that God is being referred to as what some call a "plural of majesty," meaning God is much larger than the very pronouns we use to describe him. Common in the day of the writing of the Old Testament, kings and queens would be regarded as "us" or "we" because such terms were much more glorious than "I" or "me." The writers of the Bible picked up on this and thought, "Well, God is like way more glorious than them, so let's use this interesting literary device." But perhaps most interesting is how uncreative a name Elohim is for God in this first sentence of the Bible. Oddly enough, the word *Elohim* was not a name for God that the Jews came up with. God never revealed this as his own name to Israel. So then, where did it come from?

Bible scholars believe that many ancient Near Eastern cultures, such as the Canaanites, who are discussed in the Bible, had been using the name Elohim for their gods some time before the Jews borrowed it as a name for their own God. There's evidence of this in writings and hieroglyphics. So when the Jews needed a name to refer to their God in the Old Testament, they didn't invent one; they looked at their pagan neighbors and borrowed one from them. Positively, I would imagine naming your God the name used by your pagan neighbors most certainly made talking religion much more favorable to both parties. But negatively, it also added to the confusion. Because you could be referring to "god" (Elohim) and be talking about some cult god and not the God of the Israelites. This is why people in the Old Testament often refer to their God as "the God of our father Abraham" or the "God of our father Isaac."

This was deeply practical. So we don't get our gods confused.

Lincoln Log Creation

Genesis, the story of the God with the borrowed name, continues; God invents the whole creation from the ground up, both the stuff that's up in the air, and the stuff that's below it.[3] Everything. The whole kit and caboodle. But how God creates the world in the Genesis account is surprisingly different from the way many of us had imagined he would when you observe *how* God creates.[4] Before reading the Bible, I'd always imagined that God made the world like some manufactured home in some heavenly warehouse and then just came down and put it in place on some predetermined concrete foundation. Yet when we read the story of Genesis, we discover a process that is rather unorganized, messy, and even *chaotic*. In fact, the second verse talks about how God's Spirit hovers over the "waters," or the *tohu vavohu*, which means something like "the emptiness and darkness." One translation of the Bible calls this "the chaos." Then God's Spirit hovers over the water and brings it to order.

Think about that. First, God makes stuff. Then after pulling that off, when God makes stuff he doesn't make it the way a manufactured home is made. Rather, God makes stuff *unorganized* and then spins it into meaning and beauty as his Spirit hovers over it before day one.

---

3. I love the idea of the Bible as one big coherent story. This idea is developed and expanded upon by Craig G. Bartholomew and Michael W. Goheen in *The Drama of Scripture: Finding Our Place in the Biblical Story* (Baker Academic, 2004).

4. For a very heady but helpful treatment on both the creation story and how it informs the way we live and think, read slowly William P. Brown's *The Ethos of the Cosmos: The Genesis of Moral Imagination in the Bible* (Eerdmans, 1999).

Then, out of the *tohu vavohu* God invents trees and cows and clouds and Adam. It's as if God is like a little girl. She stands above a chaotic pile of Lincoln Logs her dad threw on the hardwood floor. Then, piece by piece, she stands over it and builds and spins something majestic out of the primordial mess of little wooden pieces. It evokes the idea of possibility, of creativity, and of creativity that is ongoing: a Lincoln Log creation over Manufactured Home creation. In Genesis, pouring out the logs takes only two short verses. The ordering or the organization of it all, the spinning of the beauty, takes the rest of the Bible. So like a movie, the camera pans away from the pile of Lincoln Logs and begins to focus on a little girl who stands above, dreaming and scheming with possibility, just yearning to make something awesome out of the little logs before her. Let me introduce you to the girl.

Her name is *Ruach*.[5]

Ruach is God's Spirit. In the story of Genesis, the Spirit, *Ruach*, hovers over this primordial chaos like a little girl ready to build and construct something majestic, helping to order it all to perfection.[6] *Ruach* is all over the Bible. Throughout the rest of the Bible, there are many images of *Ruach*. A dove. Fire. Wind. Water. Cloud. In fact, one of the images of the Spirit in the Old Testament is that of the cloud.

The cloud was very important for Israel; it was the cloud that led them through the wilderness during the day just as the fire led them by night as they fled from Egypt. That meant they could never get too far ahead of God, even if they wanted to, without the chance of getting eaten by wolves in the desert. It was the cloud that *overshadowed* the

---

5. Yes, in the story of Genesis, *Ruach* is portrayed as a female character. More on this later.
6. One of the most profound books on the Holy Spirit, who is portrayed as the power and entity that holds all things together since the creation of the world, is the incredible *The Holy Spirit and the Christian Life: The Theological Basis of Ethics* by Karl Barth (1938; Westminster/John Knox Press, 1993).

tent of meeting for the Israelites when they were in the desert in Exodus 40:35. It was the cloud that *overshadowed* the temple Solomon built. It was the cloud that *overshadowed* Israel when they wandered through the desert. The cloud is everywhere and *overshadowed* God's people. So there is a very central connection in the narrative of the Bible of the same Spirit hovering over chaotic creation that similarly *overshadowed* Israel, *overshadowed* the temple, and *overshadowed* the creation of the world in the beginning. Now about two hundred years before Jesus was born, the Jewish people decided to translate the Old Testament, which is written in Hebrew, into Greek so that everyone who wanted to could read it. The problem was finding words they could use in Greek that were like the words in Hebrew. This was challenging because they are *very* different languages. It was an undeniably difficult process. They managed, and what came of it is this translation they call the Septuagint, the Greek version of the Hebrew Old Testament. And it was this translation that the earliest Christians read from, because most of them did not know the Hebrew of the Old Testament. And in this process, some hard-working rabbis, who had to find words to translate from Hebrew to Greek, had to find some Hebrew word for their word *overshadow*.

One of the words they picked to convey this image was the Greek word *episkiazō*.

Hover

Let's hover over *episkiazō* for a moment. The special thing about Mary was that she was perhaps twelve or thirteen when she gave birth to God. Talk about responsibility. When I was thirteen, I was still running up to my neighbors' during dinnertime to quick knock on the door so I could run and hide in the bushes to watch them stand in the doorframe, frustrated with butter on their chins and wiping their hands with a paper napkin. That's how I got my kicks. I thought I was pretty sly, sitting there laughing and writhing in the bush. I'm pretty sure they could see the bush shaking if they looked close enough. Compared to a twelve-year-old girl about to birth God, my childhood was a cakewalk.

Now it's one thing to give birth at twelve or thirteen. Try birthing God, as if birthing normal human babies isn't hard enough. Try birthing a member of the Trinity. Try birthing the person who invented you before the creation of the world. Try birthing the one who spoke your womb into existence. Try birthing the one who has the power to take away the sins of the world and not be somewhat concerned you aren't being a good parent.

These are real pressures.

Yet the gravity of Mary's pregnancy is actually not in three of the four gospels in the New Testament. Strangely, of the four gospels, Luke's gospel is the only one that takes the time to tell us the story of a teenage Mary getting pregnant. Now Luke, who may have been a doctor, has this whole agenda about the Spirit. In Luke 9:34, Jesus is being transfigured before three of his favorite disciples on top of a mountain. Luke writes, "While Jesus was speaking, a cloud appeared and *episkiazō*'d them, and they were afraid." This cloud from nowhere *overshadowed* them. This is the same idea we talked about from the beginning of the Bible at creation and the desert and the temple. Same thing going on. The Spirit does to the disciples and Jesus what it did to the creation in the Old Testament, what it did for Israel in the desert, what it did at the temple when God descended.

Luke doesn't stop there.

Earlier in his gospel, Luke, writing about Mary giving birth to God, says that this one time an angel came to her and that the "Holy Spirit will . . . *episkiazō* you." And when it has *episkiazō*'d her, she would give birth to God (Luke 1:35). Mary was *overshadowed*. And she gave birth to something. The Spirit hovered, *overshadowed*, *episkiazō*'d Mary. This same image is in Genesis 1, the desert, and the temple. Just like the *tohu vavohu* in Genesis, no doubt Mary was a chaotic mess when she discovered she was going to be having a baby. But the Spirit hovered over her and conceived a God within her who would eventually save the world. In the Bible, in the beginning, God watches as the Spirit *overshadowed* the chaotic world, the Spirit *overshadowed* the tabernacle in the desert in the midst of the Israelites' chaos, and in Luke the world watched as the Spirit *overshadowed* the otherwise normal twelve-year-old girl's life and chaotically made a mess of all of her plans in order to birth God. So in this faith, there is an oddly close relationship between chaos and God. The Spirit of God is either present over chaos or creating it.

Marshall McLuhan, a man of faith who studied culture as an academic, once wrote after years of reflecting on the chaos that our world has become, that to bring order into this jangled sphere, humans must find its centre (in his classic British spelling).[7] But what is the centre?

I think McLuhan understood Mary. And us. For Mary, God not only created her mess, God *became* her mess. Literally. And if Mary made a bumper sticker, it probably would have said: KNOW JESUS, NO PEACE. Mary's centre was Jesus. I'm trying to make him mine.

The problem remains the mess this inevitably creates.

The Bush

You see, for Mary the mess was intentional. She had to embrace it. Because it was God. And letting it be what it is. We must do the same, whatever the mess is, because God is in it. Frankly, I sometimes worry that people sell Christianity because they've conjured it up in their mind as this solution that'll fix the mess of our life like some kind of drug with the long commercials. Jesus becomes almost therapeutic; like a vapor rub. With few to no side effects (that we know of). The only

---

7. Marshall McLuhan quoted in the phenomenal autobiography of this British technological saint by Douglas Coupland, *Marshall McLuhan: You Know Nothing of My Work!* (New York: Atlas & Co., 2010), 10.

problem with that Jesus is I haven't met him. Yet. If that is what the real Jesus is like, I want to meet him and apply him ASAP to my messy life. But honestly, my life is way messier *after* I started following the Jesus I met than it was *before*. With Jesus, there are new questions, with new possibilities, and new potentials. It makes room for a whole new mess. The Jesus mess. Trust me, it's a lot easier to not follow a guy who says you have to love *everyone*. Even your enemies.

That's why I think the writers of the New Testament say that when people come into and experience the person of Jesus, they are a *new creation*. I think back to what creation was like. It was chaos. Then God brought the order over time. For some odd reason our idea of "new" is so messed up. New doesn't mean perfect. New means that all the building blocks for something beautiful are now there. Like a pile of Lincoln Logs on the hardwood floor in the living room. And we stand there with God above this new thing called eternal life and envision what the whole thing could look like. New means possibility. And it's with that possibility that we get to work out this whole thing, because the Spirit, God's *Ruach*, is hovering over every little piece of chaos in our lives.

You see, I think God is like a little pubescent boy. He's that kid in the neighborhood who likes to run up to your door every once in a while during dinner and ring the doorbell, only to run away and hide in the bushes. He gets so much satisfaction out of it. Watching you stand there with dinner on your face as you look for the little brat who rang your doorbell. He just sits there. Hiding in your bushes. Waiting. Smiling. Wanting to play tag. And if you look close enough, you can see the bush shaking. He's out there. Just waiting for you to chase him. Because your chaos is his joy.

Here's the point. Our lives are chaotic; a running around. Yet in the midst of it, someone keeps knocking on the door. *Hovering* to me is coming to the awareness that the person knocking on my door is Jesus, and he is hiding somewhere in my front yard, waiting for me to come and find him. The difference is you can have no vision and still have vision. You can have no idea *what* you are doing and know *that will come in time, but for now, just follow me.* Now when I dream, and pray, and hope about the future, I open the Bible and see from page one a Spirit hovering over the chaos of our world. It hovered over Mary and birthed Jesus. It descended on Jesus at his baptism like a bird. It hovered over me in my math class. And it hovers over you.

Jesus reminds me of me when I was a kid.

It's like Jesus has nothing better to do with his time than run around the neighborhood, knock on all the front doors, and run and hide in the bushes of our life, ruining dinner. We stand at the door wondering who's getting between us and our tuna casserole bake. We stand there, knowing someone's out there. Somewhere. All we know is, *someone has knocked on my door.* Jesus is your chaos. He is the one knocking at your door. Part of me wonders where he's hiding. Somewhere he is there. Christianity, although it's deeply flawed, taught me one thing. A knock at the door is often surprisingly holy. As is the one who knocks. And I think, if you look closely, you'll see what I see. What Israel saw. What the disciples saw. What Mary saw.

That bush seems to be shaking.

CHAPTER TWO

White Elephant: Messy Church

I'm a man. And this is how I got pregnant. Like a drunken lover, I fell for the Bible when I became a Christian. It mesmerized me. Initially going off to college for two years to study philosophy and history and political science at a big university, I realized it wasn't for me. Later that year, I ended up trying some classes at this local Bible college just up the road that my friend Nic told me about. It became abundantly clear to me that Bible colleges are weird places for weird people. On so many levels. There were perks. What was super nice was the girls were all like *really* ready to get married. Like yesterday.

In one of the first classes I took, there was this girl who would sit in the back of the class with me by the door. She was weird, like Bible college girls sometimes are. But she wasn't there to get married. This was refreshing. After graduating from high school, she thought God wanted her to be there. I liked that. We would sit in the back and laugh at really stupid Bible jokes we'd come up with. There was also this funny professor who had this odd way about her that always made us both laugh. Man, this girl could make me laugh. Insatiably. During mandatory chapel, we'd sit together and quietly make fun of the sermon so we could survive. We'd also write little notes in each other's Bibles under the verses, which I later learned was like grounds for excommunication. Then later, in seminary, I found out scribes did the writing thing in the Bible all the time. So I feel okay about it now. But there we'd sit in chapel and just be. It's not that we didn't get stuff out of the sermons or worshipped Satan or anything like that. It's just that there has to be some way to mentally survive Bible college. Let me repeat: *mandatory* chapels.

If you can't find some creative way to laugh your way through Bible college, you'll graduate and become an atheist. And it's increasingly difficult to get a job with a Bible college degree as an atheist, especially in *this* economic climate.

Two years later, on a beachside in Oregon on a cold stormy night, I asked the girl who made me laugh through Bible college to marry me. After our wedding, we started leading this Christian Bible study at this local college campus. These were some of the best times in our life. Our church bought this old sorority that was turned into a co-op where we would live together, eat together, worship together. Sixty of us. It was incredible—like Woodstock without the free sex or the drugs. On Friday nights I'd get up and talk about God. It was crazy. Like three hundred college students would show up. Out of nowhere. Sometimes I'd look out and see this group of really smart people who were undeniably smarter than I; PhD students, philosophy majors, dental assistants. I wondered why they came. Talking to really smart students from the university was my favorite part of being there; they were smart and had beautiful thoughts about God, and they made me rethink lots of things about my faith and life and the Bible. And it was during this time that there were some people who had math-class moments like I did. It was beautiful.

God messed it all up.

On a cold winter day, Quinn and I were walking down Belmont Street after teaching a class at a Portland university. Like it always does in Portland, it rained really hard that day. After window shopping, we thought we'd stop in for a cup of coffee at Stumptown, this Mecca for coffee lovers in Portland. We walked in and ordered some coffee, sat down on those cold metal chairs that make your back curl, and we talked. Taking notice of my surroundings, it was one of those coffee shops that make you feel cool just by being in it. You know the type: abstract art on the wall, everyone's got dark-rimmed glasses that make them look crazy smart, a soul patch, four thousand nose rings, and tattoos on their tattoos of their tattoos. Like walking into a city of John Lennons. With rain on our shoulders and steaming hot coffee, it happened. I felt something riveting in my gut. Like lightning it flowed through my wet body. I asked Quinn, "Do you feel it in here?" She said she did. Like this presence. Ominous. Powerful.

It was as if there was this weird mystical sense of God and time and space all melted into one in that coffee shop, and that something, quite unexplainable, was *hovering* over us and doing things we couldn't explain. Ever felt that? I felt, and I hate this word, *called*. It was weird, but I knew. I knew what had happened and I couldn't get away from it. No matter how hard I tried, it just wouldn't go away. It was like I got pregnant. Like an unborn fetus kicking within the walls of my soul. We went home and didn't really talk about it. But the longer we were home, the harder it was to be there. I couldn't stop thinking about the coffee shop and the people in the coffee shop. I couldn't stop waking up in the middle of the night, tossing and turning, because something was kicking in me and it wouldn't go away. Two years later, we knew it was time. We told our families, our friends, and the college group that we loved with all our heart that it was time to go. To go to Portland and be with the people with the dark-rimmed glasses, and sit in the coffee shop where I got pregnant and wait for something to happen. We didn't even know what we were supposed to do; so when people asked how they could pray for us, we always told them to pray what we were praying for ourselves.

"God, if you don't show up, we're screwed."

The Bible talks about how, when Jesus looked at people waiting to be fed, he had compassion on them. The word Jesus used for compassion literally means "in your belly." Jesus looked at the people and felt compassion *in his belly*. It's the same feeling you get when you watch TV and see the picture of little African children with no food and really big bellies with flies flying around them. Same feeling. That describes it well. It was just in my belly. Like Mary. We left the coffee shop and all I can say is it felt like I got pregnant. *Episkiazō*. We just packed our possessions, said good-bye to the college group, and moved to Portland to live in an old house down the street from the coffee shop with the nose rings and tattoos and cold chairs.

Fifteen crazy people packed their bags, got jobs, and came with us. It's the same for us all: being here hasn't told us what we're supposed to do next, so until there's clarity, we eat a meal, pray, sing songs, and read from the Bible on Sundays. The hope is that sometime as we are all sitting around talking about the Bible, Jesus, and the world, there will be this moment in our living room when God will show up like he did in my math class. And the Spirit will tell us what to do. Until then, we're going to wait. Because sometimes waiting is how to find your next belly decision.

Christians are pregnant people who understand that God is their mess.

X

You learn a lot by starting something. This was when things got weird, when we had to name the church. I've always struggled with church names. It's extremely odd to me that the further we get from Jesus two thousand years ago, the longer the names of our churches get.

Third Church of the Faith Baptist of the Pentecostal Jesus-only in the Bosom of Judah McMennonite Center of Faith.

How do you go about naming a church? Maybe churches should be named for what its members are supposed to do. I have a friend in marketing who told me he thinks people don't like church anymore because there's a massive breakdown in the way Christians talk about what the Christian faith is all about. He says people don't like church because what they end up getting is way different than what they got sold to them. I think he's partly right.

Besides the whole long name thing, it's probably safe to say there's a major breakdown in marketing for the post-Jesus church. The idea of marketing church troubles me, on many levels. Although I would imagine that marketing before Jesus died would have been much simpler, because the CEO was around and could field questions himself without outsourcing to a group of nitwit publicists who got the message wrong around every corner. When Jesus was around, I would imagine people liked being able to go straight to the top—like being able to call any McDonald's and Ronald picks up. In terms of marketing, Jesus was absolutely brilliant. He asked his followers to give up everything. He told his disciples to die. This one poet-embalmer who owned a funeral home once said that to be dead is to be spoken of in the past tense.[1]

Jesus asks people to be past tense people in the present for the future.

For good reason, people fled to and from Jesus' message. On one hand, people were drawn to Jesus' message for the same reason people were to Osama bin Laden. Both bin Laden and Jesus claimed to offer both a way to live *and die* for something in a world where no one knows how to do either with passion. They both offered a new way to live *and*

---

1. Thomas Lynch, *Bodies in Motion and at Rest: On Metaphor and Morality* (New York: W. W. Norton & Co., 2000), 35.

a new way to die. It just happens that Jesus' way is redemptive. Jesus was in-your-face about his particular kind of way. He would tell people in the middle of their workday as they fished or cooked or collected taxes, in a confident yet clear tone, "Come and follow me." Then he told them essentially, "If anyone comes after me, he must deny himself and take up his cross and die." A major difference between Osama bin Laden and Jesus is how they taught their followers to die: one for revenge, another for love. No one would come if we named our church *Follow and Die*.

It might best suit the situation to name a church after that: *Follow and Die Fellowship*. Because Jesus told his first followers to follow and die so they might live. For them, X marked the spot. From my vantage point, it would seem those lucky enough to have encountered this upstart semi-intrusive Messiah would essentially have had three choices. Choice number one: refuse to pay attention to Jesus on grounds you really liked your job and were up for a raise in the next year. Or perhaps your kid wasn't out of high school yet. Option two: listen to Jesus with a preliminary sense of obligatory openness to his kingdom venture, only to wait and see the folks he had already gathered and give a rain check on the simple basis that his current caravan didn't live up to your high expectations of what it means to follow God or have a social life. Or thirdly: you leave behind your boat, your tax collector's booth, your nets, perhaps even your family, leave everything in storage, and follow with a sense of purposeful insanity, just to have the guy you left everything for tell you to *come and die*. He'd inspire people to leave their families, their jobs, upsetting the entirety of the religious framework. Whew. You can almost hear the marketing department crank out an office-wide memo denouncing the idea. Note to Jesus: The marketing department may have a difficult time with that one, Lord.

In the end, Jesus was a brilliant marketer. For twelve radically crazy people, Jesus was their choice. The Bible explains, as well, that many unnamed individuals said no to following Jesus. As a marketer, he set the bar for being a part of his squad so obscenely high as to keep those who weren't very serious at bay. You literally couldn't follow him if you weren't serious. And this was all for good reason. Jesus expected nothing less than X from his disciples. If X marks the spot, the X for the disciples was exactly that.

Jesus' X was a cross.

Today, it's hard to sell X. I don't hear many people selling X; at least successfully. Not to their fault. No one today is buying crosses other than the ones you can wear around your neck. The types of crosses Jesus was offering don't sell in a world like this one. Our gold crosses fit around our neck. Jesus' cross took the whole body, the whole being, everything, and required a painful, bloody death. Maybe that's why people are fleeing from church. Or they may be fleeing because they are *not* hearing about it. I'm not sure. What they bought isn't what they were promised. They were promised pain-free, cross-less religion that makes everything better. So they quit because the cross they are feeling on their back is way heavier and more painful than the cross they were sold at the beginning. How can we solve this? How can we market Jesus' way more accurately? We have two options.

Flint Knives and Black Eyes

Option number one is to bring back circumcision.

This isn't my first choice, but it would get the job done. All around the world for a vast part of Hebraic history, if you become a Jew at any age, you were required to become circumcised. It started with Abraham. He's walking through the desert to go to the Promised Land, and God tells him that he and all his family and anyone else who would be with their community must cut off the extra skin on their penises. This marked their relationship and set the standard rather high for those who wanted to be a part of Israel. I'm sure Abraham struggled with this bar that God had set so high. So would we. If God had told me that, I'd have bartered with him a little: "Hey God, could you just give me a friendship bracelet or something? Let's just have a barbecue."

But God required it.

Every male in Israel who called himself by this God, must be circumcised. Whether you're born into it or you're a late bloomer. If you're collecting social security. *Every man.*

Now back on a marketing level, the brilliance of circumcision is that it keeps the lukewarm at bay. So if someone is a Jew, you know they've had to undergo the same traumatic experience you have. Talk about camaraderie. It was, interestingly, the issue of circumcision that first became the discussion of the first-century church. After reflection and prayer, for good reason, the early Christians said we should stop circumcision because people were putting more faith in their sliced penises than they were in the saving work of Jesus. It's understandable that they chose to end this practice, a practice I am thankful ended. Especially as a convert at sixteen. But on the downside, the end of circumcision allows for those not so serious to creep into the community of faith. In this way, there is a profound benefit to circumcision: *it keeps nonserious people from signing up.*

So either we bring back circumcision . . .

Or option number two.

We more honestly communicate to outsiders the difficulties of being a follower of Christ.

Recently, I went to this church service. At the end after his sermon, the pastor got up and told the people to close their eyes and pray. Then he said that all who were comfortable and wanted to become a Christian should raise their hands so he could see them and pray a prayer, with everyone else's eyes closed. After the prayer, the pastor said that for those who prayed, everything would improve and they would begin to experience a better, more *blessed* life. Then he said there was a new believer's packet at the info desk on their way out in the foyer. In a way, at the time, I thought it was really neat. Like most, I peeked. This really genuine lady in my aisle raised her hand and prayed silently and cried. *People need this*, I thought.

And I still think that was really powerful. Really. The thing that sticks out to me is how Jesus never did the whole raise-your-hand thing for his disciples. Jesus never told people to close their eyes. He tried to open them. Jesus helped people see. Why do we tell people to close their eyes? I have always wondered where the idea of prayer and closing your eyes got connected to becoming a Christian. Also, Jesus never gave them a new believer's packet. He did the opposite. Jesus gave them his Spirit. The Holy Spirit was the first new believer's packet. And somewhere along the way something changed. Because there is a difference between Jesus and the messages we sell today. What did Jesus sell?

Jesus sold death as a way to life. A long, painful death that he himself was going to model for his disciples and the world. But the Christian message today can too often sell a really quick fix: everything will be fine, life will get better, you will get richer. I fear being misinterpreted. Ultimately, at the end of the day, altar calls should continue to be done. People need them really badly. I do. I should wake up *every morning*, open my eyes, and pray the sinner's prayer. I just think that when people come forward to the front to become Christians, we shouldn't say, "Welcome and great decision. All your problems will be fixed, you will be completely provided for, everything will be awesome."

I think maybe, when people come forward to the altar, we should look them in the face and say, "Do you want to follow Jesus?" And if they say yes, we look at them with a sense of genuine compassion, and then with all of our strength, we should punch them square in the face. Then we should say, "Welcome to the kingdom of pain. This thing sucks. Hope you're ready." And we should do that because following Jesus is hard. Really hard. And that bruise on the face is the mark of discipleship, the pain, the gore, the strain and toil.

It's all about that bruise. And our marketing team needs to be more honest with new Christians on the front end about how life can suck if you follow this God. Jesus' church is a support group for those learning to live with the bruise.

Suburbs of Sodom

Being here for some time, I've found that people sometimes talk about Portland like it's a suburb of Sodom. Like it's this evil place. And Mount Hood is supposed to be a pillar of salt.

Those people don't know my neighbors.

Portland is what happens when you take Elvis, the '80s, and a love for weird and put it in the blender. Portland is where young people go to retire. I love it. I think it's a messy city and that's why I love it. The same is true of the church in Portland. It's okay that church is messy when you realize it isn't a club for the spiritually elite or a gentlemen's club for holy people. Now I see church way different than I did at sixteen. Back then I saw the pastor as this spiritual guru who spent Monday through Saturday at the park talking with Jesus, taking notes for his Sunday sermon. Now I see the humanity a little more clearly in church. Sure, that comes with being a pastor at a church, I guess. Some time ago before we moved to Portland a friend told me two things about the city. First, it has more strip clubs per capita than any city in the world. Even more than that, it is the sex trafficking capital of the Northwest because the Columbia River is a major thoroughfare where water travel and I-5, the main interstate highway on the West Coast, converge. It was the perfect place to traffic women, children, and men for sexual exploitation.

Then my friend told me something else. He said Portland has more nonprofit organizations helping people in real and profound ways than any other city in the world. I thought about that for a while. What a quirky combo. But you learn quickly that Portland is a quirky city. When we were packing our apartment for our move to Portland, we knew we would be moving to a city of paradox, contradiction, and weirdness. One of the healthiest and most service-oriented cities in the world is one of the most depressed and sexually awkward, matched by nearly year-round rain and constant mugginess. So we packed our rain jackets and Bibles and moved to Portland, not because it's normal but because we think Jesus is in a bush in Portland. So there we found ourselves and the fifteen or so other people that moved with us and chose to live near our house, where we were going to do church. That's when the mess began.

Someone once said that preaching to a pastor is like farting on a skunk.[2] Maybe that's why we have a hard time taking a hint. The mess started before we started the church. Two things kept me up at night about starting a church. First, I wasn't entirely sure what the world needed was another church to solve its problems. I remember my favorite TV host/prophet, John Stewart, once said that religion is a powerful healing force in a world torn apart *by religion*. I laughed out loud.

There seem to be plenty of churches in the world, and I was confused as to why Jesus would want us to start another one. Second, I didn't know how to start a church as no community college has a correspondence course on the topic. So much for ideal beginnings. We knew we were moving into what is called the Hawthorne District of Portland, but that was about it. There were lots of things we needed to figure out, and the first thing we had to decide was what we would name the church. I sat in front of my computer for hours to come up with really sexy names that would make people want to come. Some of them were really long names. I wondered if other people wondered why their church was named this or that. Try giving a name to a church. It's hard work. After sitting in front of my computer long enough, my thought was that if this is Jesus' church, he should name it. Up to that point, he was relatively quiet on the issue, so we just didn't name it. For eight months we called ourselves "A Church in Hawthorne." It was very literal. Now we call it "Theophilus" (pronounced kind of like "the awfulness"). Theophilus was some anonymous guy whom Luke wrote his gospel and the story of the church to. Looking back, there were

---

2. Again, in Lynch, *Bodies in Motion and at Rest*, 25.

some benefits to not naming the church: people who were mad at their home churches weren't able to Google us and find us on the Internet and come and get mad at our church when they found out it was imperfect and ruin everything and want to leave our church too. I'm glad we named the church later.

My New Guitar Pick

When we got to Portland, I thought it would be nice to talk to other pastors in the area. So I called. I didn't hear from many of them, which is fine because they are busy, but that allowed me time to have some very nice conversations with their secretaries. They told me about the pastors and their churches. Soon people in the community and in our church started asking me questions. Some of them were understandable. Others weren't. There was one question I just couldn't answer, both out of ignorance and honesty. They'd ask, "What's your vision?" I just didn't know how to answer that. Some of the books I read said people will come to your church if you come up with a compelling vision with values and mission statements. I put some of those on paper but they didn't even compel *me*. So, lacking a good answer, I went to the Good Book. What I found compelled me. What troubled me was how little time Jesus devoted to explaining to his devoted disciples how to run church services and come up with vision statements. None at all, in fact. This was problematic, especially for someone who wants to start a church, because it means there is no divinely inspired way to have a church service, or build a Web site, or write a set of values. You would think this would be something he would at least mention, but he didn't. It would have settled a bunch of our questions though.

As he's leaving earth to go to heaven, Jesus stops for just five minutes to explain to his disciples how to transition between the two fast songs and the three slow songs, how to think up a good illustration for point three of the sermon, and give them a doctrinal statement on how to do a greeting time. Something like that would have been nice, but all of it is up to us. So when the people kept asking me about my vision, I didn't know what to say. Then one day, something struck me. As Jesus is going to heaven, he says something to his disciples who are watching him rocket off to heaven. The only thing he told his disciples at the end was to *perimenein*. It means to wait. This is an odd ending to a fabulous messianic career. He doesn't talk about going door-to-door to pass out cards for Easter services or getting an AM radio station for 24/7 expositional preaching. He says to wait. Just wait. He tells them to go into Jerusalem and simply wait. And let me tell you, waiting is both painful and messy.

The first Sunday came.

We got together in our living room with those fifteen people, and a couple extra, on a Sunday evening for a meal and some prayer. After eating together for the first time, I got out my D-18 Martin guitar and played a couple of poorly planned songs just slightly off-key, sounding much more like Johnny Cash than John Mayer. Then I stood up with my Bible, hoping to preach and give hope and vision to those in the living room. But when I stood up, I completely forgot all the words I wanted to say. It wasn't like I didn't know what to say as much as I realized I wasn't supposed to say what I thought earlier I was supposed to say. So we just sat there and waited. It was awkward. Then I asked if anyone in the room knew what we were supposed to do next. After a while, my wife said maybe we should pray. I thought that was biblical, so we prayed, which made the silence holier. I opened my Bible and read where Jesus said to wait as he was going to heaven, and my wife started to cry because she was afraid of not knowing what was going to happen. Then we prayed even longer on our knees and took communion on the floor and begged Jesus to tell us what to do or we were screwed.

To this day, thinking back, it was the most beautiful church gathering I have ever been a part of since I became a Christian.

You could almost feel the Spirit hovering *tohu vavohu*. The chaos of church. It was beautiful. We finished praying and stood up and hugged each other. Then came taking the first offering. It takes a lot to run a church. Most people who start churches would have you think they need prayers and good thoughts and all will work out. Now that's true, but if you get to the core of who we are, we need cash. Cold hard cash, because we need to eat food. I like reading in the letters the apostle Paul wrote because he would tell them he needed someone to send him some food or something before he died. Missionaries need to eat too, Paul would say. When we moved up to Portland, we had no idea how God would pay our bills. So at the end of our first weirdly wonderful church service, I took this little box with a hole in it and passed it around. I told people God wanted them to give money or we couldn't make this happen. After we were done, I went downstairs to our basement where my office was and opened up the box. I was so sure God would give us enough money to make it through the month. Then I opened it. What was inside changed my life. There was $38 and a guitar pick. I still use the guitar pick. It wasn't the lack of money that freaked me out. That wasn't my first thought. I was sitting there in my basement with a box of $38 and a guitar pick, and my first thought was, *I could do anything with this money and no one would have any idea.* That freaked me out. There's no book on this stuff. *I could blow it on anything. And no one would know.*

In my downstairs office I realized I was a sinner more than ever before. And I had come face-to-face with my own selfishness. There was only one solution. So I went down to the bank the next day. Waiting in line, I told the lady at the desk that I wanted to set up a new name for our church. She opened my account and checked my identification. She asked me what the name of the church was. I told her our legal name, which at that point was still really generic. And I asked her if there was a way I could set up our account so people could write checks to another name other than our generic church name. She told me we were allowed one DBA. A DBA is a "Doing Business As" name, where people can write checks to one other name and it is credited to your account. She asked me what I wanted people to be able to write their checks to. So I told her. She had to ask her manager if she was allowed to set it up as such, which turned out to be surprisingly okay. She asked me why I wanted that name, and I told her it was so that every time I opened the box with the hole in it, I would never forget what I was looking at. So that I would never think this was money I could do anything with. It was a name people could write on their checks so that I could remember who I was. She changed our name and said good-bye.

Now people don't write their checks to us. People write their checks to *Jesus*.

Now when I look in the little box, I know whose money it is and that my job is to treat it as such. I have a great bank that lets us have a church that can receive checks in the name of God. Deposits are sometimes awkward. But at least I'll never forget whose money I am handling.

By far the messiest part of our church is the meal. At our church, we eat a meal together before we worship in song and read the Bible. I like it because it forces people to get to know each other beyond the "turn to your neighbor" moment of the church service. We think that if someone has to say "pass the salt" or "can I have a napkin," it will drastically increase their chances of getting to know their neighbor and of eventually living in community. We also feed people at our church so that, literally, no one can say they aren't getting fed. This has been important for us since day one. One time a man without a home walked by as we were eating together and we brought him in and fed him. That was the most effective church service we have ever had. After we had started meeting for food, worship, Jesus, and the Bible for some time, I'd reflected on the whole "vision" thing people were asking me about.

I started to look at how Jesus formed community around himself, and it was surprising how many times in the Bible Jesus is found eating with his disciples, and tax collectors, and prostitutes. This truly is the eating God, and part of discipleship is "pass the salt." People around me

are always saying they are leaving the church they go to because they
aren't getting fed. I don't know what that means exactly. No one in our
church can say that because they have garlic on their breath. "I'm not
getting fed" was never uttered by Jesus. Jesus didn't go to synagogue to
get fed. He went to feed. And because Jesus didn't go to church to get
fed, we shouldn't either.

That's why I go to church. There are hungry people at church who
need me to come and help them. Frankly, there is so little at church
I hunger for anymore. Sermons don't speak to me anymore, worship
songs aren't as tear-jerky for me, and the greeting time is glossy and
uncomfortable. That is all okay with me. It really is. I'm also done
complaining about it. Because it isn't about the sermon or the songs,
or the glossy greeting times. We go to church to be like Jesus, to do
for others what he has done for us: love our neighbor. I go to church
because I want to help people like Jesus helped other people. And
that's why Jesus never said, "I'm just not getting fed there anymore."
Jesus went to church to feed people and cast out demons. It's become
increasingly odd to me that those who actually give the most are the
ones who complain and gossip the least. The inverse is equally accurate.
Those who never give are the ones that gossip the most. I would
suggest there is something very powerful in that. Human beings are
programmed to be happy when we give more than when we receive. At
least that is what Jesus said. You are more blessed to give than receive.[3]
The fabric of America is weaved with the opposite of that. The point is
that Jesus' church is messy like the chaos at the beginning of the Bible.
Ultimately, every church group that says they are different than the rest
is lying to themselves and to the whole world. They are no different.
They are full of the same kinds of people: people who had nothing
better to do than leave their nets and tables and lives to follow Jesus,
bumbling along by faith.

---

3. Acts 20:35.

The community of Jesus is the group of people who say their lives are beyond help and are so messy, all they have left is a little faith in a maniac who apparently didn't obey the rules of death. It is a community of faith. No wonder we run from church to church looking for something else. Maybe the problem isn't the church. Maybe the problem is what we are looking for. We have traded a community of faith for a community of everything else. A community for conservative Republicans. A community for old people who hate loud music. A community for people who hate gay people. All of these other things. And they are all the wrong reasons for us to gather. We gather because of Jesus and our inability to save ourselves. A friend of mine said that is what the gospel is: *Jesus eating really good food with really bad people.*[4] Nothing else. All of our other gospels are not gospels. The gospel that says our prettiness is what impresses God. The gospel that says we can do this or that for God and he will finally love us. The gospel that says if we can make the religious *GQ* next month, we are fine. All of these are different gospels. And they are all like imitation vanilla extract. They smell like heaven, but they taste like hell. They're nothing more than an extract. An extract of something real.

Wait

All of this is why if I were to write a book on how to do church, it would be about why people who are going to do church should not read the books on how to do church.

Few of these books say what Jesus said to do. When Jesus told his disciples to do church, he said one thing: wait. There are some great books out there on how to start a church, but some of them give really bad directions. They say if you do A, and you start B, and you have

---

4. Len Sweet continues to put ridiculously important truths in very memorable ways. This point is made excellently in Leonard Sweet, *Nudge: Awakening Each Other to the God Who's Already There* (Colorado Springs: David C. Cook, 2010), 174.

program C, then Jesus will show up and all the people with money will come and you will be fine. But it requires you to do A, B, and C. Mess any of those up and you mess up your future as a successful church planter. The problem with those instructions, although probably good ideas, is that none of them are what Jesus said to do. Wait. Wait for what? The Spirit. It will come on you, and then you will go. But you can't go until you stop and wait. The greatest enemy to waiting on the Spirit of God to come in the way the Spirit wants to come is A, B, and C. A, B, and C are fine; you just have to wait until after you have *perimenein*. Something really sad to me is that we teach people that God is A-B-C. That's a linear God. Nothing in all creation is linear. Everything is curved.

A hero of mine, Dr. Brunner, my church history professor from school, once told me that it's possible to start a church without God. What he was saying is it's easy to think if you do A-B-C like those who know what they are doing in all their books, then thousands will come to your church and give money and you can hire more people so you can get more people to come. They are just steps, guidelines, or principles. And A-B-C are good sometimes, don't get me wrong, but only sometimes, only after you *wait*. Hear what God is saying and do it. If you don't hear anything, keep waiting. Another thing. Wait on Jesus to say something before you run to another church to try and fix your problems. Wait on Jesus before you get cynical. Wait before you quit. Because when you wait, you can see something hovering. The Spirit amidst the chaos. And in your midst you will find hope. Wait. Sometimes when we wait in the middle of our pain we find the hope and grace we need to bear with one another in love. Sometimes acting in pain perpetuates it.

Recently, the questions about our vision continued. Someone sent me an e-mail and asked, "What's your vision for the church?" I stopped, looked at my computer screen puzzled, and wrote back, "I don't know. You're asking the wrong person." He said, "Who should I ask? Do you have a Web site?" I told him, "The person you need to talk to about that question doesn't have a Web site." They said, "How can I get ahold of him?" I told him to pray. Perhaps no greater challenge for those in the church is discerning what Jesus' mission statement for his church is. So few people seem to be asking this question today; I still think it is a very important question. I had a dream once that our church would have a Web site. Under "Vision Statement" it would say, "Whatever Jesus said or did." Then, under "Mission Statement," it would say, "See Vision Statement." Then, under "Values," it would say, "See Mission Statement." If you are mad at church, or about to quit, stop looking for your church to give you a mission. Start practicing the things Jesus did at church. Probably no one will follow. That's okay. You aren't called to have disciples. Jesus is.

White Elephant

Sometimes people come to church just to watch me talk. I hate that. I judge those people a little on the inside because they are wrong. They don't get it. Not to mention it makes me self-conscious. Like a potluck, being the only one to bring something is rather anticlimactic. I admit, learning to make sense of the mess that is church is overwhelming at times, let alone contributing and participating. Many of my friends have given up on trying, mostly because they don't have anything to contribute in the community of faith that they have been a part of. I told one of those friends that church is like a white elephant party.

A white elephant gift exchange is this brilliantly ridiculous party during Christmastime where everyone brings some piece of unneeded crap that has collected dust for some period of time in the corner of their attic and gives it away as a gift. Figuring out what to give for this type of exchange can be stressful. This one time I decided that I would give away an old box of sensitive medical documents that I had saved over the years with information about my eye exams, vaccinations, blood tests, so on and so forth. I put them all in one big box, sealed it up, and took it to the party. I've been to lots of Christmas parties, and most of them are the same: karaoke, cookies with the little green sugar droppings, candy canes, and a really skinny Santa. None of them compared to this white elephant gift exchange. Imagine it. People fighting over the most useless stuff for the sake of fun. Everyone wanted my box of sensitive medical documents. My friend Dan has them today. I don't know if he has read them but if he ever does, I hope he still wants to be my friend. But what a blast. What a blast to make a gift out of some of your trash. A white elephant gift exchange is me seeing my trash in a new way, as a gift, as a contribution, as something of value. What we think is trash becomes a gift. And that's what I think the church is. Some call it mass. I call it mess. Potatoes, potahtoes.

Idolizing the Ideal

Now that I have been a Christian for like twelve years, I think I would like to go back in time and tell myself something to save a ton of pain and heartache: *lower your expectations of people and church.* We begin to see the Spirit at work in the church when we choose to take our idealized views of what church should be—with all of its holy trappings—out into the backyard and shoot them between the eyes.

When we idealize community, we idolize community.

And when we idolize church and community, we forget the one who formed it. At the very place we make the church to be the club of the pretty people, we create and imagine something that exists neither in reality nor in God's imagination. It's weird to me. I have never heard anyone say about their AA meeting that they aren't getting fed. There are two reasons for that. First, they don't go for a product; they go for the friendship. And second, that's because they have really low expectations of those who are showing up, because everyone, from top to bottom, is an alcoholic loser. I wonder if people go to church and "don't get fed" because they don't so much see themselves as losers, but they see everyone else there that way. Our expectations of church will *always* lead us to cynicism. You can't be cynical when you realize you are simply one of a bunch of losers. Ask why you go to church and you will find out why you are mad at it and are becoming cynical.

Often during the life of St. Francis of Assisi (1182–1226), a phrase would be written over the doors of the churches. It said *Domus Mea*. In Latin that means "My House." Francis was one of those other weird kinds of saints. He was raised in a pompously rich family, at one point was employed as a playboy, and then felt the call to leave his evil life behind to preach. Every one of his possessions was sold or given away except for the shirt on his back. Francis is famous for running naked through the streets out of protest. Many within the church thought he was a nut job. As time goes on, he grew increasingly disenfranchised. Who wouldn't? Then one day something changed. At a run-down chapel in San Damiano, at a crucifix that had escaped decay, he heard Jesus say to him, "Francis, don't you see that my house is being destroyed? Go then and rebuild it for me."[5] After that, he occupied himself with repairing the chapel until he died in 1226. This affected his entire life. Francis was a man who grew increasingly frustrated with all the trappings of church. He was frustrated with the hypocrisy. He hated the greed. He deplored the institution. But he didn't run. The story of why he stayed was told:

> Francis recognized that without the Church there would have been no Mass that February day. Sinful though it was, he was entirely devoted to [the Church], for it was the guardian and repository of a tradition that had to be kept alive. Francis had none of the smug superiority with which some people consider themselves outside and above a sinful Church, for he

---

5. Donald Spoto, *The Reluctant Saint: The Life of Francis of Assisi* (New York: Viking Compass, 2002), 69.

was all too aware of his own frailty. In any case, he could never have conceived of abandoning the church, which had never, during his youth, abandoned him. One might say that he took it seriously but not too seriously; it was the footsteps of Christ that he sought to follow, not the lead of any churchman, cleric or saint.[6]

You see, for Francis, this was the sinful church within which he was at home. If there were a sinless church, he could find no fellowship there.

Remember this: being the church is like finding your X. It's painful, but it's the spot. Jesus called it a cross.

---

6. Ibid.

CHAPTER THREE

Brazilian Hospitals, Pregnant Women, and Butter Dogs: Messy Prayer

Trust is what God resurrects when our security dies.

My friend Phil knows something about this. He's a missionary. Although Phil is not one of those missionaries who goes to Mexico during spring break to build a house, or feeds the homeless downtown one time during Christmas break. Phil is no *occasional* missionary. He's one of those missionaries who lives and dies to be overseas all the time: bus rides, Spam snacks, prayer for the sick, smuggling Bibles. That sort of guy. Being a missionary is Phil's life. Phil is crazy ADD. He can't sit still; like one of those people who sits for five minutes and starts shaking his leg uncontrollably, like he's got a disease or is about to explode of some internal boiling anxiety. For Phil, life is a reason to go anywhere but here. I love that about him. It just makes me insanely jealous, because his stories are way better than mine. He comes home on what they call furlough every once in a while. Furlough is when a missionary gets a break. When he returns from a trip, his stories are palpable with intensity, with life and death around every corner; soaked in faith and prayer like one would imagine the life of a missionary would be. We listen with our jaws at our shoestrings. People getting healed. Pagans turning to God. This sort of stuff. We hang on his words.

But I remind myself that Phil is only *one kind of missionary*. You see, I used to think the life of a missionary must be an insane venture—a mixture of passionate Bible preacher, fearless intrepid traveler, with all the qualities of Indiana Jones. Missionaries were preachers plus archaeologist, without all the women and drinking. I would think it was the life of a backpacker always hoping for some kind stranger to take the missionary in, and after a night of earnest discussion, the unsuspecting stranger ends their life of doubt and understands perfectly Jesus as their personal Lord and Savior, becoming the next indigenous missionary to their pagan homeland. And that might happen. Really. It might and I'm sure it does. It just hasn't to me. Neither to Phil the missionary.

Phil tells me that the real God stuff for a missionary isn't always what they do when they get to their destination, but rather what happens on the way to the mission field. He also tells me that God sends missionaries so he can whip the missionary into shape. Sure, God uses them in some distant village somewhere. But ultimately God sends a missionary into the middle of nowhere so he can spend some quality time with the missionary. The missionaries come back changed. They believe in God more. They love people more. They were the ones who met God. Imagine that: missionary needing God. That's why Phil likes being a missionary. Not for the adventure. Not for the travel. Not for the jaw-dropping ministry he does. He goes because *he* wants to find

God. I'd never thought of it like that. I pack up, get on a plane, get a host family, and hope to go and be some apostle-like knight who brings Jesus to a dark and musty pagan world. Now, after being on five mission trips, I've learned one thing. At the end of the day, *I end up becoming a Christian all over again.* The people that go find God afresh. They have an altar call in a foreign land. The missionary needs the new believer's packet. The people they go to serve end up teaching them more than they could ever imagine. Phil says maybe missions is more about the missionary than anything else. Phil is more right than he knows.

I've tested this theory.

Some years ago, I'd been invited by a friend to come and speak in Brazil at some churches where they spoke in tongues and "Amen-ed" in Portuguese through the whole thing. From a local college where we served, we took ten students to Brazil for a week to do whatever the churches needed us to do: work, paint, preach, whatever. My friend Joachim, who was from Brazil, was going to be our translator because our team didn't know Portuguese. After a ridiculously lengthy flight, we arrived safely in Rio de Janeiro. We saw the Brazilian beach, spent time with Christian communities throughout the country, and walked the Rio de Janeiro strip late at night. It went oddly smooth. But that's just how God works. He leaves the worst for last sometimes. On our next to last evening, we were all settling in to go to bed when we got a call from Joachim at midnight saying that one of the American girls with another host family, Alise, was getting very ill. One of my Brazilian friends drove me down to the house Alise was staying at. I was hoping nothing would really come of it. I was way wrong. Something was *very* wrong. After going to her room, the first thing that was clear was that she was whiter than a ghost, vomiting out her ears, and had passed out once already. She was a trooper though. She just sat there with this odd smile on her face like nothing was wrong.

Now, I didn't go to medical school. My medical training amounts to little more than years of observing *Grey's Anatomy* and Dr. Huxtable.

But I knew something was quite wrong. We all got into a van and drove down to this little tiny hospital in the middle of this tiny little town in the middle of nowhere, managing not to let Alise pass out again on the way. I remember that drive very clearly as we drove the streets of that Brazilian town through the night. I remember thinking about the worst case scenario. I remember thinking about having to tell Alise's mom that her daughter was really sick. Now, to be honest, pastors are not people who like to be honest about such feelings, because we are paid to trust in God. We are supposed to be beacons of hope and faith, never concerning ourselves with the worries of life. On the outside, I was fine. I was like, "Alise is fine. Let's all just pray and trust." But on the inside, I was like, *"She's got Ebola!"* I didn't want that on my record. Having a missionary die on your watch in a foreign land isn't something that comes off your pastoral record very quickly.

As we neared the hospital to rush our wounded missionary in to be helped, I realized that this was one of those moments in my life where I was entirely and completely and without qualification, *out of control.* Nothing I could do could make this better. Nothing. We pulled up to the hospital. It was when we drove up that I knew this was going to be one of the longest nights of my life. In front of the hospital doors were these two dogs that were so dirty, they looked like they were covered in butter. *Butter.* We put Alise into a wheelchair, and I had to kind of kick the butter dogs out of the way in order to get into the emergency room. As we walked in, the hospital waiting room was so full, you could barely fit another person inside. Not to mention the fact that there were like four hundred pregnant women in this hospital room, all in about their thirteenth month of pregnancy. It was a crazy scene.

We quickly learned that the doctor didn't speak English, so Joachim our translator communicated for us. I sat with Alise out in the waiting room to make sure she was okay. And sitting there, in the hospital with the butter dogs, next to the exploding pregnant women, with a doctor who didn't speak English, it happened. Ever have one of those moments in your life when Jesus chooses to speak to you at a time outside the fifteen minutes you gave him earlier in the day? One of those moments where something is so incredibly clear you have to sit down to take it in—like a sunset that you never thought was possible. I sat there. And Jesus told me something. Something I'll never forget.

Jesus gets a kick out of moments like these.

Don't get me wrong. Jesus doesn't enjoy watching people get stuck in little Brazilian hospitals. It would be challenging to believe in a God like that. God never takes joy in any needless suffering. For his disciples though, something inside of me suspects that moments like this are at the center of his plan. Chaotic, messy moments when we're totally not in control are just his batch of tea. Jesus gets a kick out of stuff like this. Because in moments like this something is waiting to be birthed. Trust.

A Scientist Gets Lucky

Ultimately, it turns out that Alise needed some hydration. Nothing an IV and a long nap couldn't fix. *Close call.* We stayed with Alise in that Brazilian hospital with the butter dogs and the pregnant women until the sun came up. Walking slowly into the fresh morning sunlight, Alise learned a poignant lesson on the importance of water. And I, one on trust. It was burned onto my mind: *Jesus gets a kick out of moments like this*. Because trust is what God resurrects when our security dies. It is at the very place where we are entirely free of security and guarantee and predictability that we're all on the verge of trust. But it's during the three days of death when the tomb is still full that we really get freaked out. Christianity offers us a brilliant insight into those sorts of messes. That maybe death is no more than the sunset of hopelessness, and resurrection the sunrise of hope. We call this God's kingdom.

That's the beauty of God's Spirit. It is the God here and now in our messy midst. Maybe, when the Spirit whom Jesus sends comes and lives in us, we don't have to go overseas to be a missionary. When this God sets up shop in you, going to the store is a mission trip. Getting your hair cut is a mission trip. Going to a movie is a mission trip. Because Jesus said that this kingdom is "inside of us." The Phils still need to go overseas. Don't get me wrong. But each of us walks and breathes as missionaries where we are. Right where you read this. You are a missionary. And we are all on a mission trip. There is no furlough for being full of God's Spirit. What if people that trusted Jesus were the most hopeful people in the world? They trusted in each other. In God. In grace. In hope. How would the world look different? How would we look different? What if we defaulted to trust as opposed to fear?

Trust is the poison that kills monotony.

NPR gives the liberal in me a reason to get up in the morning. That would have been more difficult to admit ten years ago. Back then, when faith was relatively new to me, I'd study the Bible in one hand and change the channel to Fox with the other. I like NPR now. Not for the politics or the weeks they have to raise money. NPR rocks because, along with the weird shows, they produce shows and stories about things that make me think. There was this science show last week that covered how they found a satellite that's hovered around the moon for like twenty years. They said it found a little patch of frozen water. Right there on the moon's lunar cheek. Real, fresh and wet, earthy water. The kind that could support life. You can imagine how ridiculously cool the scientist felt who found it. The hot lady scientists looked at him differently after that, I'm sure; standing around and gawking from the water cooler. They probably threw him a space-person party. Whatever that would look like. What's weird about finding water on the moon is how it's been there this whole time. It was just under the surface. Being a disciple of Jesus is like finding water on the moon, like finding something that has been there this whole time. It's not a discovery or invention of something new.

As a disciple, you don't invent anything new. You just discover what's new *to you*. Something they never saw before. This whole time it's been there like a hiding puddle of frozen water on the moon. Christians aren't any more pursued by God than pagans or Hindus or Hitler. It's not that God loves them now that they're finally on his team but hated them before they obeyed. That's ridiculous.

Finding Jesus is like finding water on the moon. It's simply choosing to stop ignoring the love that has been around you this whole time—*a love you just didn't see.* It's putting on 3-D glasses and seeing your story in a completely new light. It's seeing the world differently because you have new eyes. If you want to trust in God, you need those new eyes. This kind of awareness destroys our false sense of independence. It ends our individualistic sense of power. It says, this whole time, from birth to now, *someone* has been personally making your heart beat. *Someone* has been giving you food to eat. *Someone* knit you in your mom's bursting womb. *Someone.* And it wasn't you. The idea of God says that even if you think you can control all the variables in your life, save enough for retirement, get perfect grades, never go to jail, make millions, at the end of the day, *someone else makes your heart beat.* You can't do that one on your own. When I tell my friends about Jesus, it's like telling them about water on the moon. Christians give something away that people already have; they just don't know it. Christians just tell people they need to stop ignoring it. And there's a party around the water cooler when you find it.

Trust

This wild sense of trust we've been discussing is the primal operating system of Christianity. Let's go back to the idea that the entire Christian faith is built on the notion that trust comes when security dies.

The church was built on this notion. Paul, the murderer-turned-apostle, who essentially started most of the churches after Jesus ascended to heaven, was perhaps the worst pastor in the world. On Paul's missionary treks, he'd roll into this town or that town late at night after the bars had closed when everyone was in bed. Then he'd preach the next day, get death threats from religious leaders, start a church in someone's home, and narrowly escape in a couple of weeks.

In fact, he rarely stayed anywhere. His longest stay in any city was something like three years. *Three years!* And that was the longest. That's a short tenure to pastor any church. Most of his surviving letters preserved in the Bible were penned either on some horseback, in some dark prison, or in the dark little corner of someone's basement he'd crashed in for the night. He didn't have time for a study or a quiet library. These letters were written in between doing ministry.

All of Paul's letters were written in the context of personal chaos.

So after starting a church, they'd write him a letter asking him questions about the very faith he'd just sold to them: How do we do communion? Is Jesus coming back? Can we still get drunk? All of these, though, were questions he had to answer from a distance. So much of Paul's ministry was done while he was absent. He was the most absent pastor in the world. This was, and is, the most brilliant move in the world. Paul could have started one church, stayed, grown it to be a megachurch, and been invited to speak at all the best pastors' conferences. But he didn't. He started a church, brought people to faith, then left. Right away. Then he'd write letters to help them out. But he had to be gone. It was brilliant because, had he not done that, they would have done to him what we do to pastors today. They would have started to worship Paul instead of Jesus. In Paul's absence, they had to trust in someone else. The Spirit that now lived in them. The Jesus that saved them. The Father that sought after them. You can't have real trust if you are looking for a pastor to be a god. Put it this way: half of trust is dismembering old trusts. It's stopping our trust in dumb things. Stop treating your pastor like Jesus. Stop waiting for a Paul to come and fix your life and start talking to the God who lives in you. God is omnipresent. Your pastor isn't.

Pants

Christian spirituality is the act of letting God wear the pants in the relationship.

From page to page and story to story, Jesus invites people to this new kind of relationship. These people were called *mathētais* or "learners." Sometimes we call them *disciples*. Jesus' method was quite impressive really. When Jesus would invite these *mathētais* into a new relational context, he is recorded as uttering to each of them the word *akolouthei*. *Akolouthei* was this word that beckoned men and women to leave everything they had to follow. It meant *come and follow*. In one of these stories, Jesus, walking as he always does from place to place, bumps into a tax collector named Matthew. Matthew hears Jesus say *akolouthei*, abandons his tax-collector booth, and follows. The next sentence in the story really makes little to no sense. Jesus says come follow me, then *in the next line they are having dinner at Matthew's house with a ton of sinners and tax collectors.*

Now that to me is a radically large jump in the story. I'm not the sharpest cheese in the fridge, but how'd we go from "Come follow me" to "Can I come over and have dinner at your place?" My only explanation is this: Jesus is like almost every college-age person I've ever met. College people are unflinchingly gifted at inviting themselves over for food at any home that has it. Imagine it: after inviting Matthew to follow, they're walking along and Jesus turns to his new friends and quietly says, "Hey, can I come over for dinner?" Because for Jesus, being invited to follow means you're cooking dinner. This story tells me two things.

First, if we are called by Jesus to this trust thing, our trust will always cause us to hang out with people we would not normally like to hang out with. Awkward people. People with different theology. People of a different orientation. People of different denominations. The Bible calls them "sinners." Notice that the word "sinners" is almost always in quotes in the Gospels. If we are disciples, the people in the quotes become the people we are called to eat with. A friend of mine once told me that the gospel is Jesus eating really really good food with really really bad people. The second thing is this: Jesus is the sort of guy who invites himself into our personal lives and borrows our stuff. In the New Testament, he borrows someone's colt, someone's donkey, someone's boat. Then he invites himself over for dinner.

Given this passage in the Gospels, we can't invite him into our hearts, because he's already invited himself over for dinner. He's like that.

In the Bible, something momentous has stayed with me as I've read these brutally honest stories about this famous carpenter/convicted-felon/God-man named Jesus from a little town called Nazareth, famously unknown to the God-raising business. What's stayed with me is that either Jesus, in all his apparent wisdom, decidedly and intentionally chose the saddest and slowest morons available—on purpose—as the future of his upstart globe-shaping organization, or he's the sort of carpenter/convicted-felon/God-man who's surprisingly difficult to keep up with. Because as you watch, so many of these stories are about these people called "disciples" following Jesus, who over and over *aren't able to keep up with this guy*. Ultimately, my gut says both are true: that this Jesus from nowhere is significantly faster than his disciples, who, if we're honest, are slow yet faithful morons. At the end of the day it makes for a fun story. Disciples slow. Jesus fast. This stuff sells itself. I know no other religion that portrays a god who gets dust in the eyes of his followers; followers from nowhere, of nothing, and rather slow. Followers who fish, willing to leave the day job to learn a new way to fish. I know no other kingdom where a nothing fisherman from Galilee becomes the first pope.

The Jesus in the Bible is constantly at least one step ahead of everyone else. It's everywhere in the Gospels. For instance, the gospel of Luke doesn't advance more than two chapters before Jesus gets lost from his parents at the temple in Jerusalem. The story goes that Mary and Joseph accidentally leave him behind at the temple, nearly sixty or so miles from home, at probably thirteen or fourteen years old. Realizing he is gone, they run back, sweating, reeking of BO and shame, with a blush on their face that would make my "ruby red" crayon jealous, to pick up their God-child they abandoned at the temple. Finally, as the text says, after *days of looking*, they discover him at the temple discussing God with scholars and Bible teachers way outside his theological pay scale. And his parents can't help but note they are all astonished at him. And the little kid goes on to explain he was supposed to be there the whole time because that was his, quote, Father's house. Mary is just glad they found him. But Joseph stood there, looking confused. Probably at least a little perplexed.[1] If God doesn't have permission to bring over people we don't like, I wonder if we are trying to wear the pants.

From Yes/No to Why/Why Not

If we're going to possess the willingness to let God wear the pants in this relationship, it's going to have to begin with how we talk to God. In our communication skills. Have you noticed these really long commercials for medicines and drugs that keep finding their way to our televisions? You've seen them, hurting and ailing people surrounded by dark clouds and lightning who, after a dose of Fixitall, are perfect happy people running on the beach with their dog on a beautiful sunny day. (Warnings: *Fixitall is not recommended for those with genital herpes, diabetes, heart conditions, or a clear conscience. Please consult with your doctor before using.*) Glued to the TV, we are left believing all of this is possible if we ask our doctor about this or that. If only you had this or

---

1. This story in Luke 2:21–52, in my opinion, is one of the greatest evidences that the New Testament is inspired. It is so ridiculously honest. Jesus was a kid when this happened. He would barely remember, and for sure wouldn't know the embarrassing story of how his parents actually found him. So who passed the story on? Probably Mary, or Joseph. And if I were Mary, this would be the last story I'd want passed on, let alone put in the Bible. My point: no other religious book in the world is more honest about the stupidity of its heroes than the Bible. Ideas for further honesty: Adam, Eve, Joseph, David, Solomon . . . everyone in the biblical account.

that pill, you'd be *this* happy. If you ask me, this is the most brilliant form of advertising in the world. Prompted by the power of suggestion, people go to their doctors and pressure them to prescribe whatever heart, herpes, or happy medicines will do the trick. The patient transforms into marketer to their doctor. Then the doctor becomes the jerk if he or she says no. Brilliant. It wouldn't work if the pictures of the people in the commercial were all depressed, alone, or crying, would it? You can't sell over-the-counter drugs with pictures of people not fixed by them.

Unless you're Christianity. Christianity markets a method of talking to God that *doesn't solve all their problems.* This form of talking and listening (we call it prayer) often creates more problems than it solves. But it works. To build muscles, people lift weights. To find love, people go on dates. To grow trust, Christians pray. Nothing else builds trust quite like facing all of your ongoing problems and unsolved struggles by getting down on your knees and not trying to fix them the way you would your gutters or broken refrigerators. In this way, prayer is trust in the form of silence and contemplation and honesty.

The idea of prayer in the Bible is perhaps way different than the other religious traditions. It says that when we don't know what to pray for, *God actually prays* on our behalf. What other faith buys into the idea that God prays for them and listens to himself? I think it's a stellar and profound idea. Now, this also assumes Christians are the sort of people who don't have fabulously eloquent prayers. This is the sort of movement for those whose prayers are wildly boring. Maybe in other people's religions if their prayers aren't good enough, the gods won't hear them. In this movement, the Jesus one, God spots those who don't have the strength to lift up good enough prayers.

When I was in college, I picked up this little book about how to have good body posture when you talk to others. I think the title was something like *Body Posture in One Minute.* For a book on interpersonal communication, it was a horribly written book. But it taught me almost everything I know about prayer. The book talked about when you talk to people and meet them for the first time, most of us start our conversations with closed-ended questions that don't spark conversation like "Are you good?" "Do you have a job?" "Are you going to school?" Then the book said the best way to be good at the art of conversation is to *ask more open-ended questions*. It will always spark better conversation. Open-ended questions require the other person to talk more about themselves, giving them space to be vulnerable, honest, and real. And most of the questions that do that begin with the words *how, why,* and *where*. Sometimes when I pray I feel like God is not speaking to me. I should say, most of the time. At all. But when I read that book, it became clear to me. When I pray, *I only ask God closed-ended questions*. "God, can you provide for me this month?" "God, give me patience." "God, I need forgiveness." When I read that really bad book on conversation, everything started changing.

Now I have experienced that when I open up and ask God open-ended questions, it gives God much more of an opportunity to talk. "God, why am I so worried about my savings account?" "God, where are you?" "God, how are you going to forgive me?" If the Bible is right about something, God has more words than yes or no. He has a fully formed dictionary and can talk. We talk to God as though he knows only two words. Ask God bigger questions and you will find bigger conversation a reality.

The kind of conversation we are speaking of began in Eden. To be sure, it's almost certain that God didn't invent the garden because he needed more vegetables. He invented the garden and put Adam and Eve in it because he wanted someone to walk around with and talk about vegetables. "God, how did you invent carrots?" "How'd you pull that whole sunset thing off, God?" The garden is about friendship, not farming. God could have simply invented a carrot if he was hungry. God's invention of the garden was simultaneously the invention of prayer.

Prayer, I guess, is a result of eating the fruit in Eden, isn't it?

Before that, prayer consisted of nothing more than coming out of your tent right by the avocado trees and walking up to God by the river and saying, "Hey, wanna go swimming?" I think that was the sort of thing God was after when he started the world. Afternoons with Eve and Adam. Just being together in the river by Eden. Soon though, eating the fruit forced their modes of conversation to change. It went from face-to-face to eyes-closed-for-a-minute, ending with an amen and "in Jesus' name"; like a married couple deciding to relate only by tweeting each other through the day. What a sad replacement. Swimming with God in Eden to formulaic statements. Sometimes we sound so entitled when we pray, like God owes us something. Prayer is not me being God's accountability partner, holding him to what he said he'd do. God doesn't need an accountability partner. He invented accounting. For me, trust begins in prayer, where I'm forced to learn to simply be content with the one who has junk figured out. The Bible says that the first Adam led us all into sin. The Bible also says that a second Adam came who would redeem everything. His name was Jesus. Jesus came to redeem and turn around all the ridiculousness that the first Adam created. It is implied in the Bible that the second Adam got done everything that needed to be done. No one else could do what he did. Prayer is practicing the realization that you are not the third Adam. Someone else already got the stuff done that needs to get done.

The First Awkward Small Group

Why, I don't know, but praying with others has always been incredibly challenging for me. Perhaps more than most, I was a special-wants child: son of a rich doctor, brother of none, living in the rich white suburbs. Spoiled is my maiden name. This makes prayer surprisingly difficult, as it never pans out on the terms I had desired. I must have a disease. I can't pray with my wife most of the time. It's weird to pray with the people who know us the best. But that's okay,

I think. After Jesus resurrected, the first church service is a prayer meeting. Jesus has just gone to heaven and told his disciples to go into Jerusalem and wait for him. Then they all go together into Jerusalem *and start to pray*. They must have interpreted waiting as praying. But there was apparently a secretary there, because the story in Acts tells us who was at that prayer meeting. It says the disciples, Peter, and Mary the mother of Jesus were there. Now that wouldn't be that profound had it not been forty days earlier that Peter, this Rock of a man, the man upon whom Jesus would initiate his church, had denied Jesus. Three times. Now, at the first prayer meeting was Mary, the mother of this Jesus.

Catch this. The first prayer meeting after Jesus ascends puts Peter, the guy who denied Jesus, in the same small group as Mary, the mother of the guy Peter denied. Talk about an awkward prayer meeting. But what a *real* prayer meeting. If Peter were here, he would most likely admit those were some weird prayer times. "Jesus (*Crap, Mary knows what I did. I'm sorry*), we love you. Amen." It would have been darn near impossible, because Mary knew all the dirt on Peter. He couldn't pray big, illustrious, and sexy prayers. *She knew what he did*. Communal prayer is authenticated when the person you are praying with knows all the dirt on your life. *All of it*.

Almost every spiritual person I respect says that the hardest person in the world to pray with is a person they are closest to. This is verifiable by my own experience. As a pastor, I have the spiritual gift of eloquent prayers. I can pray prayers from the pulpit that make God quiver. I can get on my knees with someone in their need and sound so incredibly spiritual. Really. The problem with my wife is this: she knows all my pastor prayers really well. And if I ever try and pull them out for our prayer time when we go to bed, she will turn over, look at me, and say, "A.J., it's just the three of us. Stop your pastor prayers."

It's humbling.

Then I read that story about Peter and Mary praying together, and it all became clear. *Real prayer is when we talk to God with someone who knows all the dirt on us.* Then we can enter in. Mary knew Peter's foolishness. Quinn knows my pastor prayers. She knows my mistakes. She knows my history. And we pray together. If you are finding that you don't want to pray with the people who know the dirt on your life, then you are running from the type of prayer the church is formed on. Real prayer happens when in the back of your mind you keep thinking, *This person knows just a little too much about me.* Or you can put it another way. New Testament prayer never happens outside the context of relational intimacy. Jesus taught his best friends about prayer. Even the Lord's Prayer is about intimacy with the Father. If you want to learn to pray, find someone who knows you really well, and get on your knees with them and just be honest with God. If you want to develop a more real prayer life, stop praying your pastor prayers and pray with your greatest enemy. Pray with the one who knows all the dirt. Now when I go to bed and pray with my wife, most of our prayers sound something like this: "God . . . *help!*"

Sour Cream and Waldo

Prayer, ultimately, is taking the time to allow the God that is under our nose to be given space to speak and be.

Ever stand in front of the fridge looking for the sour cream only to realize after twenty minutes of looking, it is right in front of you? Trust is like that. It is looking for something that is right in front of us. All we have to do is *open our eyes.* The sour cream is there. So is God. Trust is sour cream. It's the thing that is right under our noses that we can't see.

I saw a Where's Waldo? book at the store the other day. There are lots of Waldo books. He's a tricky little bamboozler to keep up with, isn't he? No wonder there are lots of books about where he is. Where is Waldo? The first question in the Bible is oddly similar to that. God asks Adam in the garden, "Where are you?" It says that out of fear, Adam was hiding from God in the garden. The first question God asks in the Bible is oddly similar to the question most of us are asking of God right now. Lots of my friends are asking where God is. I am. My wife is. Where is God? The difference between God and Adam is that God doesn't hide when we ask the same question. Ever looked at a Where's Waldo? book and taken note of the scenes Waldo finds himself in? Weird pirate hunts. Civil War battlefields. The pictures are always so incredibly chaotic. And then you find this guy in a striped shirt standing right there in the middle—just standing straight and smiling at you awkwardly the way a criminal would look in a mug shot. Waldo is creepy. But he is like God. Prayer isn't getting God into your picture. Prayer is knowing in the chaos that there is a guy standing there smiling weirdly at you. *With* you. You just have to find him. He's there, in that book. I promise.

Prayer keeps the book open.

CHAPTER FOUR

My Old Man's Drunk Again: Messy Family

Christians are like pagans. They believe in a God that can be touched.

Like demonic possession, I remember the moment puberty entered me. It was in sixth-grade gym class. We were climbing these big ropes and there, across the gym, was my first real crush. Her name was Carri. Before puberty hit, I'd never really paid attention to Carri. Girls never really drew my attention. And then puberty hit and everything was different. I remember looking at her this one moment in gym class and all of a sudden, this foreign and life-altering primal emotion took over. I had never felt this odd alien feeling before. So there, standing in my tight Adidas gym shorts in sixth-grade PE staring at Carri, I heard puberty whisper to me in its new evil voice: *Huh, that's different.*

Moments like these make you question the very fabric of the universe, don't they? Like Copernicus audaciously telling us the Earth isn't the center of the universe. Everything I thought I knew changed.

Puberty makes me wonder about Jesus.

We say Jesus was God. Then we say Jesus became human. *Entirely* human. Now on one hand it seems like a real move down to me, from God to human. One of the angels should have hinted to Jesus, "Don't take the job. The pay sucks. They're going to kill you. You'll have to go through puberty." I'm sure one of the angels did. You'd hope God has friends like that to tell him this sort of stuff. But if he did, God didn't listen to those friends. Because this God seems to be the sort of God who likes to move down the ladder of success for the greater purposes of redemption, to die in our shoes. But on the other hand, it makes me wonder if Jesus had his gym-class moment like me. If he had his first crush. If he knows the *Huh, that's different* moment when puberty attacks. Ultimately, this idea of God becoming human is a hopeful one for all of us. Because if Jesus became human, then Jesus is the eternal proclamation to the world that God understands exactly what it's like to go through puberty.

Background Checks

Like all of us, Jesus had a history. *Real* human history, with puberty and crushes and stuff like that. This is the sort of stuff he didn't escape one bit, as if he had lived in a vacuum of objective sterility free from the constraints of human fleshiness. We call this his *incarnation*.[1] He

---

1. One of my favorites, and most widely underappreciated, on the topic of Jesus' incarnation is Dietrich Bonhoeffer, *Christology*, trans. John Bowden (New York: Harper & Row, 1966). Previously published as *Wer ist und wer war Jesus Christus?* [*Who is and who was Jesus Christ?*], Hamburg: Furche-Verlag, 1963, reconstructed by Eberhard Bethge from class notes from a course given by Dietrich Bonhoeffer at the University of Berlin in 1933.

had—long and messy—a history like you and me. You could touch this God because he was as much flesh as he was God. This has interesting implications. God dirtied a bunch of overpriced, clean Jewish diapers. He woke his young mother, Mary, up at three in the morning for a midnight snack and a little comfy cuddle. Mary got frustrated with God-baby. Someone had to teach Jesus how to go in a toilet and not on the carpet.

There's a real *fleshly* history there that is central to Jesus. Initially, some bothersome problems arose for Jesus because of this important reality. Because if God became human, he did so electing to have to go through potty training. God didn't become human as a thirty-year-old, post-pituitary Savior. He endured *it all*.

The most difficult people for Jesus to convince of his cosmic redemptive message were those who knew his fleshy human history. These are the *people he grew up with*. The first time Jesus travels home after his whole coming-out-of-the-closet-as-Messiah thing, his hometown of Nazareth sees him for the first time in his new messiahship. Imagine the tension. Most definitely, it would be similar to going to a first class reunion. At my ten-year reunion, I felt rather sheepish the whole way through. Everyone else appeared to have accomplished so much more than I. *Bank executives. CEOs. PhDs.* It felt like I lived in a van down by the river. At class reunions, everyone tries to show everyone else up to prove they've got it all together more than the rest. And so you show up, all buzzed to show yourself off in all your newfound glory, making an epic appearance about all you've done since high school. *Graduated from college. Made tons of money. Have four kids in TAG (talented and gifted).* Jesus couldn't do this.

When Jesus goes home for the first time, did he show off all his accomplishments? It would have been a quick conversation. He shows up, and seeing his childhood friends, he says: "Finished my master's degree, learned how to fish, found out I'm in the Trinity." The kid he sat next to in third grade looks blankly at Jesus. He thinks, *This guy's lost it.*

Oddly enough, it was Jesus' human history that made it a daunting challenge for people to accept him as Messiah, Savior. So much so that the story we are speaking of says he could only do a few miracles there. This was the problem. Because people couldn't forget the diapers. They couldn't white-out the potty training. He experienced it all; and his childhood friends knew it. Maybe that's why the Bible really doesn't include these stories about potty training and breast-feeding. Because humans, in their closed-mindedness, find it difficult to worship and pray to someone who wet the bed. I get it. It's weird.

On the flip side, because of these stories Jesus gets humanity in a really special way that the other gods can't. Prayer is way easier when you know you're talking to someone who, like you, got in trouble for peeing on the sofa and not in the toilet. I can pray to that guy. It's stuff like that God gets because of Jesus, who is God. But that is unlike a big reason for our inability to get him. It's the very beauty of God in the flesh that makes the gospel, the story of Jesus, so intriguing. Isn't it? Because God in the flesh has experienced the worst of everything we have had to experience. Jesus, as this flesh-God, is the proclamation that at one time and at one place, God experienced puberty. He knows what it's like. I can follow this guy because he gets me.

Jesus can be a real hope because he had a family too. Now, families are central to the story of Jesus. But not in a way we might think. Two of the gospels (Matthew and Luke) start with stories about family that serve as introductions to his life and ministry. But they are both different stories highlighting different families. Jesus apparently had two families. Although there is one thing that is the same. Matthew's family tree begins with Abraham and Sarah. Luke's gospel begins with the story of Elizabeth and Zechariah, who would be the parents of John the Baptist. Both couples have one thing in common. *Both of them were infertile.* The story of the incarnation, at its core, finds its roots in the stories of two couples who couldn't have kids on their own. Now they finally did. But Abraham and Sarah couldn't knock it out of the park until they were in their nineties, and Elizabeth and Zechariah were very old as well. So the story of Jesus begins with two families. That is, two families that were impotent. It's interesting, isn't it, that the story of the guy who called himself Life begins with two stories of impotence? In the story of Scripture, it takes an infertile village to raise a potent Jesus. Not a village of really fertile people. Ultimately, in the overarching story of the Bible, the most important kids are the ones people can't have on their own. Only God can have them. Through infertile people from the Fertile Crescent.

I like Matthew's family tree of Jesus the best. Matthew includes all the religious all-stars: Abraham, Isaac, Jacob. Then Matthew, apparently unwilling to white-out the unpleasant parts of his tree, throws in Jesus' great-grandma. Her name was Rahab. She was, in the much earlier book of Joshua, a prostitute. This means a background check on Jesus would show some questionable people in his family tree. Matthew continues. One of Jesus' great-great-grandpas couldn't keep his pants up. His name was David. These are interestingly honest inclusions, aren't they? So already in one chapter, Matthew, walking us through the genealogy of Jesus, is telling us the life of Jesus begins with impotence, transitions with a prostitute, continues with sexual addiction, and ends with a virgin named Jesus. Like many of us, Jesus' family tree is riddled with a lot of sexual weirdness. His family sexual history was caddywampus at best.

A cursory glance at the life of Jesus reveals something else similar to most of us. Where is his dad? Like for many people my age, Joseph seems to be around at the beginning but then disappears by our teenage years. And of course, maybe—yes, some have thought that maybe Mary and Joseph got divorced. Others think Joseph died around the time Jesus was a young adult or got some disease and slowly perished. And knowing our culture, probably the next big hit to come out will be *The Joseph Code: Joseph, His Wives, and the Downfall of the Fabric of Family*, retelling the story of how Joseph ran off with some herd of prostitutes and started a weird cult in Latvia. All that is interesting and possible, believe you me.

But the Bible gives little to no explanation as to his absence. Joseph just isn't around. And of course, many of us look at this and are saying, "Jesus' dad was God." No doubt, I'm not arguing that. Thanks for the obvious. But in terms of a loving, caring, around-the-campfire sort of dad—farting and laughing, building forts and fishing the streams, an in-the-flesh dad—Jesus didn't really have one. And the only pictures we have of Joseph are before Jesus is born, at his birth, and in the early chapters of Luke when Joseph and Mary *lose Jesus* and have to go back to Jerusalem to find him. Doesn't sound like a great rap sheet for ole Joseph. Now to give some credit, Joseph could have been one of the greatest fathers in the world; we just don't know. But I take so much comfort in the fact that Jesus didn't apparently have that; he didn't have the ideal childhood. I really take that to heart. Why?

Few of us, at least those who are brutally honest with ourselves, know what it is like to have a perfect childhood. And maybe, just maybe, it isn't entirely necessary to have a great home life to be a great person. And maybe the greatest people in the world are birthed and born in places of pain and anguish. And maybe there is hope for a man like me to grow up and be a great husband and father despite the model I was given. Just maybe.

Like this girl I know. There's a girl who lives in our community named Hannah. She grew up in a home of atheists. In high school, she became a Christian and wanted to move into our community but couldn't even visit until she was eighteen because her parents would not let her visit a church until she was of age. And since she wanted to follow Jesus, she was obedient to her parents and waited to be able to go to church. Now we live with her. What I've learned from Hannah is that in the story of following Jesus, our redemptive future is never dependent on a ridiculous past. Hannah is growing and becoming one of the most beautiful people I have ever met. So many people like Hannah come from homes where they are not encouraged to live a life of beautiful faith in Jesus, which always makes me angry about those people who do that to them. It's very easy to take it for granted. But then again, when you live in a home of Christians, it is easy to believe that your faith isn't yours but your parents', so I guess both are equally dangerous. Christianity should always be a movement of adopted spiritual orphans. Maybe it can become a place where a raised atheist can become a beautiful Jesus-follower.

> = <

This whole idea of incarnation that we've been discussing—of Jesus knowing what it's like to be human and actually being human, and of us not knowing what it's like to be God—is really important to the conversation about family. This idea is utterly inseparable from the Christian story. God gets puberty. Not just puberty, but every single aspect of the human experience. It reminds me of what my math teacher taught me a long time ago. Remember the three signs > , = , and < ? These symbols tell us if something is greater than or less than something else. They are often used in algebra.

$1 > 0$ (one is greater than zero)

$1 = 1$ (one equals one)

$0 < 1$ (zero is less than one)

This is a way to think about Jesus. Think about this. Jesus was a human. And Jesus was the God of the universe. He also washed his disciples' feet, putting himself under them to serve them from below. That's a lot of angles to get humanity. Jesus is above, with, and under us. It means:

Jesus > you

Jesus = you

Jesus < you

St. Augustine in the fourth century used to say that God is closer to you than you are to yourself.[2] Jesus gets *everything* about you. It means every little tiny aspect of humanity, God gets. But it means every huge aspect of being God we will never understand. And that the sorrow you feel, God feels way more than you do. That the love you feel for someone, God feels even more than you do. And he gets your family more than you do.

"Biblical" Family?

Recently, a story was told to me about a teenager in our church community who said we were his only family, and without us he didn't know how he'd survive. We were family for him. *Literally*. He had no one else. No brothers. No sisters. No mom. No dad. Even his grandparents were dead. Later that day, the weight of what he said dawned on me. It made all the really mundane complaints about church life go away. Like the silliness of someone whining about the music being too loud or not getting fed by a sermon. When we realize this is *literally* family for some, it becomes utterly ridiculous and selfish. Our "sound" preferences and addiction to expecting our pastors to be a "god with a small *g*" are absolutely and minutely unimportant compared to a family for the family-less. But then maybe those who find their entire experience at church to be about the sound or the sermon don't see this as their family. And maybe those who need a family are simply looking for people to *be* with. I can understand that. I just hope the ones who don't have a family don't meet the ones who already do have a family and hear them complain about the sound or the sermon.

Some purveyors of religion claim there is in the Bible this core

---

2. Every interested follower of Jesus owes it to the faith he started to read the life and story of this man St. Augustine (354–430). The best biography I have read thus far is Peter Brown, *Augustine of Hippo: A Biography*, new ed. (1967; Berkeley: University of California Press, 2000).

message about what a family is supposed to look like. They claim this idealistic "biblical" family exists that looks a little too much like *Leave It to Beaver.* And if we could just model our families after this "biblical" family, we'd all be happier for it. I thought I would go and look for said family. What I found disturbed me to my core. The way I perceive Jesus' perception and teaching of family has changed somewhat in recent times. From my experience, almost nothing of what Jesus said about family will *ever* make it to a Focus on the Family conference, will *ever* make for a great "round the fire" story time, will *ever* make sense. Jesus said, "If anyone comes to me and does not hate his father and mother, his wife and children, his brothers and sisters—yes, even his own life—he cannot be my disciple." He also said that because of his kingdom and the exclusive allegiance to him that it requires: "From now on there will be five in one family divided against each other, three against two and two against three." And then he says, to the double take of his physical family, "Whoever does God's will is my brother and sister and mother."[3] Put *those* verses on your refrigerator.

Jesus had little to no interaction with his dad, Joseph, mostly because he was running around telling everyone he had another dad, *Abba.* You've got to imagine that made Joseph, his earthly dad, feel kind of excluded. Did he have to explain to his neighbors at BBQs and PTA meetings, "Yeah, he thinks he has another dad. We're working on him. He's in counseling."

For Jesus, the kingdom of God actually ran *against* family life at times. It's refreshing, isn't it? That the messy parts of Jesus' family tree are included. That families are anything less than perfect in the Bible. That Jesus didn't have a perfect family himself. It's refreshing. There is no religious book in the world more honest about the downfalls of its heroes than the Bible. Like the story of Noah.

---

3. Luke 14:26; Luke 12:52; and Mark 3:34, respectively.

Red-Stained Teeth and the Lesson of Grace

Noah got his job because God was mad at the world. After making everything, God saw people starting to act like monkeys, and he didn't like it. When God sees this, the King James Version (1611), not known for its shyness, says God *repented* of making the earth and its inhabitants.[4] An idea similar to this is the notion of humanity repenting. Human beings, depraved as they are, are called, from the garden on, to "repent"—in the Hebrew, *shuv*. Like when you play that game Hot and Cold. Someone is trying to find something and you stand and watch, knowing full well where the thing is they are looking for. Hot. Hot. Warmer. Cold. Colder. The idea for that game came from the Bible. To *shuv* is to hear God say, "Cold. Cold. Colder," and you then go the opposite direction until you start hearing the voice say, "Warm. Warmer. Hot!" God looks at the world and starts saying, "Cold. Cold. Colder." And so God *repented*.

There came a point, after years of watching the people he'd created, when God decided he was largely disappointed with the way it had all turned out. The story in the Bible appears to show God almost in distress over his disappointment. So after thinking about his options and feeling sorry about the whole thing, God looks down on the earth and finds someone he likes who can play the superhero to rescue the whole thing. His name was *Rest*. In Hebrew, they called him *Noach*, or as we know him, Noah.

Interestingly, whoever wrote Genesis was privy to the information regarding God's feelings, because it says that God saw Noah and thought to himself that he was the most righteous man in the world. The Bible will depict for us what is going on down here on earth, and then give a little emotional commentary on how God is feeling about the whole thing. And the writer of the story in Genesis, who can tell

---

4. "And it repented the LORD that he had made man on the earth, and it grieved him at his heart" (Gen. 6:6 KJV).

what God is feeling, will include that in the story. This took place even earlier, when God looked down on earth and was rather disappointed. Perhaps with no sense of hyperbole, the author of Genesis 6:5 says that every inclination of everybody's heart was evil. And God was ashamed. So God developed a plan to fix it all. His plan was unorthodox and probably wasn't in his initial playbook. It had never been done before. It's called a flood—a natural version of the "start over" button. But even in the midst of his frustration about how the whole thing turned out, he wanted and desired the human race to continue.

Through righteous Noah, his surprisingly willing family, and a bunch of paired-off animals, God can redeem it all. When God thought Noah was the most righteous man in the world, out of a sea of brokenness, they talked. God told him he wanted him to build a boat that could hold lots of animals and his family, because he was going to destroy the earth by a flood. Because Noah either had a great relationship with this voice in the sky or he was extremely gullible (we don't know), he did what the voice said. He built a boat. How he got the money, the wood, or the animals, we don't know. No doubt his neighbors took note. And the city planners; you need permits for these sorts of things.

Noah had three sons that came along. *Ham, Shem,* and *Japheth.* One day it started raining . . . and it kept raining . . . raining . . . For a week he'd been waiting, but now Noah knew this was it. He had already put his family, his three sons, tons of pets, and his future in the boat. No doubt his sons revered him. For years, sitting around the dinner table, Noah would tell them how this voice in the sky was telling him he would save the world. What kid wouldn't look up to *that* dad? Other kids at school were like, "My dad's a doctor." Another was like, "My dad's a policeman." Ham, Shem, and Japheth were like, "Our dad'll save the world." So they got in the boat. It would seem everything was happy to this point. At least the Disney version would have you think that. The more gruesome details are intentionally left out, except to imagine the scene when not only the downpour from heaven began but all the springs of the great deep burst forth. The neighbors come over and knock on the side of the boat, and scream to be let in. They see grandparents floating in the water. Yes, all the gory details the Bible is kind enough to leave out, but I'm sure actually happened.

One day it stopped raining. The flood started going down. Slowly. "Rest" and his boat finally came to rest on some mountain somewhere. No one really knows where. Noah gets out with his family and the cooped-up animals inside, and they started life all over. What did Noah do after the flood? He started a garden. And he planted grapes in the garden. Why not? Some people believe that Noah before the flood was probably a winemaker, hence his quick decision to pick up his old occupation. He had no choice because no one was hiring. Or rather, there was no one. And so he planted grapes. And if you know anyone who makes wine, it takes some good time to make grapes good enough for wine. Maybe ten years. After some time, he makes some wine from the seeds he brought on the boat from his earlier life. The text says of Noah, "When he drank some of [the vineyard's] wine, he became drunk and lay uncovered inside his tent."[5] *Naked*.

The whole nakedness thing is super important here. Because in the Bible, nakedness is always—*always*—equated with one thing. Shame. Embarrassment. Brokenness. It is always equated with shame. *Except for one place.*

Remember when the garden was created and Adam and Eve ran around naked with God? And remember how the story tells us Adam and Eve were naked *but not ashamed*? That is the one place shame and nakedness are not the same.

The Tent

Back to Noah, who is now lying naked and ashamed in his tent. The first son, Ham, runs in and sees his old man naked. But why?

_____

5. Genesis 9:21.

Ham gets a bad rap here. Not to mention his name is Ham. This is why we have hotlines. For names like Ham. Ham reacts as many of us do when you see your dad naked or in his chonies in the morning, making coffee on his way to work. We run. The other way. To a quiet distant solace called our room. This is a universal reaction. Every child has an allergic reaction to the mental picture of their naked parent for some odd insurmountable reason. It's universal. I would suspect the sort of thing that made Ham, the first son, run out of the tent was not the disgust of seeing his father naked. It was for another reason. I've had friends who have seen their father do something that really scarred them. One told me how, when he was a kid, he walked in on his own father looking at pornography in his office. My friend told me, aside from being disturbed, that the one thing he can't escape is the image. The picture in his mind. This is the guy who taught me how to shave. This is the guy who played Santa. This is the guy who kisses my mom. These moments are like seeing a movie star you have worshipped your whole life and quickly finding out they won't give you an autograph and actually turn out to be real jerks. It is taking something you have idolized and covering it in mud.

It's painful. Because your understanding of the very fabric of your life has changed. Everything becomes different. When Ham was a kid and came home from school, you have to wonder if his dad talked to him about hearing God speak to him while he was out in the field. I bet he did. Didn't Ham help build the boat? Didn't they have dinner at night together? Didn't Noah tuck him in and tell stories about the God of the universe? Then to walk in on him naked, drunk, and smelling of old wine. *That's* why he bolted out of the tent. The shame. The nakedness. The embarrassment. For the most "righteous man" God could find to be found *unrighteous* would be hard for any of us to experience. This exact thing happens when we find out a person of deep spiritual influence in our lives does something bad. A pastor coming out about a porn addiction. A mentor running off with the secretary. An elder stealing money from the church. This is the guy who taught Ham about God. What would you do? Run out of the tent and tell everyone else. And that's just what he does.

The other two brothers, Shem and Japheth, hear their brother running out and shouting something about their dad. So standing outside, learning of their father's disgrace before Ham, they have a choice to make. But what they do is so beautifully redemptive. Shem and Japheth go into one of their tents and get a blanket. Then, while Ham stands by and watches, they approach the tent *and walk in backwards with the blanket around their shoulders.* Then, having shielded their eyes from their father's nakedness, they cover him, walking forward out of the tent. The whole narrative ends with Noah waking up, hung over, and realizing what happened. The story ends with Noah cursing Ham's son Canaan and blessing Shem and Japheth.

What is your tent? And what are you bringing into your tent? Where are you face-to-face with disgrace? We either bring in grace or judgment. For some of us, our tent is church. Are we bringing in a blanket? If it is family, take in a blanket. If it is work, take in a blanket. This blanket is grace. It is the same blanket Paul talked about. He said that we were to clothe ourselves with the Lord Jesus Christ.[6] He was talking about grace.

Sometimes my Christian friends have a hard time loving their family members who don't identify with Christianity. And sometimes my non-Christian friends have a hard time loving their Christian families. It doesn't matter. Because real love is nondenominational. It doesn't require church attendance. It doesn't require that we agree. That's how Jesus worked. He found the most revolting, disagreeable twelve folks he could and made them his disciples. I support a lot of people who aren't Christians. People tell me I shouldn't do that because then

---

6. Romans 13:14.

I am supporting their lifestyle. I'm not sure about that. God gives me food, water, and air every day, and I'm pretty sure he disagrees with me 99 percent of the time. Love and grace don't require agreement. It requires a blanket. It requires love.

But you can't give a blanket away unless you have one in your tent.

My Dad's Dad

It was around my birthday in March, and I got a phone call on a Saturday afternoon telling me that my grandfather had died. We tried to get a plane, couldn't, then my wife and I drove to Montana as fast as we could in the midst of a snowstorm. When we got there, they told me that he'd had a heart attack when he went to put something in the mailbox. On his way back into his house, he had a massive heart attack and died that night. When we got to Billings at 9:00 AM, after a long evening of energy drinks, I got to see my grandfather in a casket. My father got there just after I did. My dad, who had always really, really loved my grandfather, had a moment to be with him alone while he lay in the casket. I secretly watched.

My dad got down on the ground, face-to-face with my grandpa, grabbed his hand, and told him he loved him. Over and over. Tears streamed down his face. I felt a little guilty for watching but knew that this was a holy moment God desperately wanted me to see. And I realized, despite all my father's problems in life, he was still a person, a human being, who had the capacity to love very deeply. I remembered how he had moved away when I needed him most. And how he and my mother never worked out. I needed to see my dad in front of that casket. Not because I'm morbid or something, but God wanted me to see my dad like that: broken, sad, depleted. After he stood up, I went to my father and hugged him. I told him I loved him. And then I knew I could love my dad for who he was and *stop judging him for who he wasn't.*

Jesus smuggled grace into our tents. Now we smuggle it into others'.

I'm not saying we need to presumptuously tell people about Jesus if they are not willing to listen. In fact, you don't even have to talk about God to talk about God. When I read the book of Esther in the Bible, I found out that God's name isn't even mentioned. Never once.

But it's still all about God.

CHAPTER FIVE

Little Bunny Foo Foo Sees a Counselor: Messy Sin

Some bunnies really need an intervention. The fairy came down lots of times. Over and over, from what we know. But Little Bunny Foo Foo kept being a moron. He didn't listen. Just kept on running through the forest, bopping mice on the head. Finally the fairy had enough. Then the bunny listened. Now those field mice can rest at night. But it took some time to change.

So do we.

Conversion might take a second. But salvation takes a lifetime.

Mark

It's difficult to discern on the spot what to do when someone says the s-word during their baptism.

Mark was mentally disabled. We all loved him

very much. Before we'd gather for worship, he'd show up on his little Huffy bike with his really big red helmet and two big flags like those that sand buggies use to make sure they don't hit each other as they go over a hill. Bringing his bike inside, Mark would sit at the same place every week by the snack table or a girl. Everyone in the church knew Mark; he had the most distinguishable laugh you'd ever heard. It was painfully loud, like a deer giving birth to a black bear or something like that. *It was undeniable.* Not only that, but he'd laugh at all the wrong moments in our worship gathering. I'd be up on the stage praying or serving communion and Mark would all of a sudden start laughing from the back. People coming up for communion, I'm pretty sure, thought some guy in the back was demon-possessed.

Mark was one of those mentally disabled people who knew he was mentally disabled and used it to his advantage. He'd come in and laugh loudly every week under the guise of "forgetfulness" or what he called his "special problem." It was so endearing. It got to the point, though, where it had to be explained to him to not be laughing during the sermon or the public prayers. One night, after laughing the whole way through the gathering, Mark pushed people aside and ran up to me after the service. He told me that he wanted to become a Christian and get baptized. After explaining to him that we didn't have a baptismal tank and that we'd have to fill a horse trough in the backyard, he insisted we still do it.

It was January and very cold. *Very* cold. But Mark was determined. So Mark, myself, and two hundred fifty college students went into the backyard in January to see the loud, mentally handicapped laughing dude get baptized. After putting on some shorts, we both got into the water. Asking him in front of everyone present why he wanted to get baptized, Mark made a beautiful confession in his undeniable scratchy voice: "I want be Christian." So we both got down in the water. I told him to cover his mouth with his hand so he didn't drown. And with everyone watching, dunking Mark in the water, I said: "I baptize you in the name of the Father, the Son, and the Holy Spirit." Mark goes down into the frigid water, ascends into the chilly January air, and screams at the top of his lungs. Now, what he said I am not allowed to write in this book. The publisher wouldn't let me. But with everyone around the horse-trough-turned-baptismal in the backyard, Mark inaugurates his new Christian faith by screaming: "Oh s——, that's cold!" Mark came up out of the water. I thought maybe I should baptize him again. But instead, we all clapped, hugged him, and welcomed him to the community.

What do you say to someone when they are baptized? Congratulations? Job well done? Way to die symbolically? None of these options seem to fit in any way, because the idea of baptism carries with it the notion that you have actually accomplished nothing. Except for dying, which at the end of the day isn't much of an accomplishment. If we said to those being baptized what was really happening, theologically speaking, parents would write us letters of concern. Imagine hearing, "Now that you've symbolically died the most horrific execution earth has ever invented, similar to that of a messianic upstart from Nazareth in Galilee named Jesus, I metaphorically raise you from the graven tomb as portrayed by these deathly waters." Home video *that*.

But usually, because we don't normally sit around and think about this sort of stuff, we're inclined to simply say, "Congratulations." And why shouldn't we? Someone said congratulations to me when I was baptized because there's no script for this stuff. But when I say congratulations as the person ascends from the waters of baptism, something feels a little off. Simply put, baptism is the idea that we have died. Died with Jesus. We'd never congratulate someone for dying, would we? You can't *earn* death. What's there to congratulate? Saying congratulations at a baptism is as ridiculous as saying "I'm so sorry" to a new mother. Now of course I agree, baptism is a huge decision, and decisions are celebrate-able with passion. No doubt. Break out the tater salad and Oscar Mayer wieners.

There are always moments for celebrating decisions. But when we congratulate people at their baptism, we unconsciously do something I don't think we want to do. It sends, well, mixed messages. In a way, without thinking about it, it trains people from day one to conceptualize their Christian faith in terms of deeds, and doing stuff for God's attention, making it all about what they've done to make their God really, really happy with them. But that's not what this thing is all about. Because, sadly, for those expecting congratulations from God on their accomplishments, there are none. Baptism is, above all, *the death of accomplishment*. There's no congratulations for dying in this kingdom. Even if we never made a mistake, we couldn't ever make this God love us more than he already does. Which leads to a profound reality.

If we can't make God love us more by doing really good things, then we can't make God love us less by doing really bad things.

The Lie

Truth, it seems, gets warped over time. It's much easier to sell a message that God loves us more when we do good religious acts to make him happy. It can drive so much of what we do. Mark Twain used to say that a lie could run around the world before truth could even get its pants on. Our messing with the good news of Jesus will always be susceptible to lies. There was this practice in the early church that may seem really odd but illustrates my point perfectly. Often people would not be baptized until they were on their deathbed. And they did this based on the idea that there was no forgiveness for sin after baptism. Constantine, in the fourth century, wasn't baptized until the day he died because he believed that way. And if you sinned, *even once*, there was no grace.

Now that may seem ridiculous. But it is no different from you and me thinking that God is *more* in love with us *because* we got dunked in water. Or haven't sinned for three days. Or don't cuss anymore. Back to what we say at baptism. "Congratulations," we say. As if to say, "You did it!" Free love from God now. We turn this into a pattern. Later, after baptism, we add to our list of *things we have to do to make God happy that day*. This usually has to do with joining the greeting team or being nicer, or reading our Bibles every day (all good things). While being deeply important parts of life, it comes across as: do this religious action = God is extra happy with you.

Again, in baptism, while I think God does rejoice, it's definitely not over *our achievements*. Point-blank, again, baptism is the end of all spiritual achievement. It screams, "I can't do it, so just kill me!" So many are drawn to Christianity for this very purpose, because at its core it offers a paradigm of love for those who have tried to earn it and realize they just aren't good enough. Christianity celebrates and redeems ugly things like a cross. Cross, the most horrible form of execution anyone could invent, with all the blood, is the thing that gives life for Christian spirituality. Baptism, the ritualistic reenactment of the burial of Jesus after crucifixion, is how we introduce people to the Christian faith. How morbid is that? But how beautiful. Yet despite this all-encompassing love, well-intentioned people keep right on thinking they're in the Jesus club because of their baptism or their good deeds, or getting all cleaned up. This is American capitalism marries cross. And it's a marriage that will always end. For Paul the apostle in almost all of his writings, this is a match made in hell.

The idea that we are accepted by grace but continue through doing good to make God happy is rather odd and quite wrong. If I had a penny for everyone who left the Christian faith because they felt like they couldn't measure up. That is interesting to me. People leave for the very reason Christ came. To end all that stuff. In a way, I kind of feel bad for God, who can't even give us something beautiful and meaningful like baptism or good works to do without us turning it into some kind of attempt to prove to God how spiritual we are and to fill up our card for Jesus. God is in a tough place. As if God is more pleased with us if we have the ability to put on shorts and get dunked in water. What kind of God is that insecure? I have a challenging time imagining a God whose love is entirely off the table unless we get in some shorts and get put in water. But that's what we've kind of done. There are whole Christian communities that say, in order for the God of the universe to fully love people in the person of Jesus, they have to get baptized. This is so dangerous.

It is striking, isn't it, that the churches that tell us one must be baptized in order to be saved also tell us we must be baptized into their church? That is brilliant marketing. Horrible theology. And not gospel.

Baptism is an absolutely brilliant form of initiation in that it requires one thing: someone else to do the baptism. Unless someone is willing to help, baptism doesn't work. *You can't baptize yourself.* It's neither biblical nor safe. It requires someone to bring you out of the water. How symbolic is that? There are two parts to baptism: the falling into the water and death, and the raising out of water into life. Only one of those two can you do on your own, the falling into the water part. The second, of course, is rather difficult to pull off on your own. Baptism is the acknowledgment that you can die on your own, but *you must have someone else bring you out of the water.* And as you rise out of the waters of death, you celebrate a new life that God brings. A new life free of sin. The s-word.

Categories

Chet. That is, the Jewish notion of sin. The s-word. *Chet* is understood to be in terms of missing the mark (in archery terminology). When we think about it, this assumes that there is a mark—a good/holy/right way to live. The Jews claimed that, no matter who we are, we all missed this mark. For the Jews, *chet* is the human condition. There is a right way of life that we *all* have missed. When you think about it, the only commandment in the Bible we've actually managed to obey is the first one. *Be fruitful and multiply.* We've nailed that one.

The rest, we've struggled with.

So in the context of all of this missing of the mark, how does God posture himself? Jesus was unique because he boldly claimed to have solved this human condition. But how? There are many good and helpful theories out there. Here's one way to think about it. Like today, during the times of Jesus, there were whole categories of people. At the top were the rabbis and religious leaders. Then there were the unclean: the Gentiles, the tax collectors, the "sinners." There were other categories too. These categories were constructed by the religious in reference to one's faithfulness to said religious leaders' understanding of this right way of life. The clean were living rightly. The Gentiles were far off. The unclean had some cleaning to do. Ultimately, these categories were absolutely central to the fabric of religious and popular culture during the life of Jesus. Now, because these categories made things clearer and safer, it was *very* important that people hung out with others in their respective category. The clean hang with the clean. The rabbis hang with the rabbis. The unclean hang with the unclean. The tax collectors and "sinners" hang out with tax collectors and "sinners." At the top were the rabbis and religious leaders, and lumped together at the bottom were the tax collectors and "sinners." These were seen as the worst of individuals. Tax collectors were seen as being in the lowest category because they were Jews who were employed by the Roman government to collect taxes, thereby further funding the Jewish oppression. This was seen as a dirty act of betrayal. Likewise, a "sinner" in the time of Jesus was someone who did not live the more popular understandings or traditions of Jewish law as described by the Pharisees, Sadducees, and teachers of the law. The term "sinner" had really almost nothing to do with living out our immoral acts as much as it did with not living up to the highly specialized theology of righteousness that the religious elite had constructed. And so the tax collectors and "sinners" were people judged for who they *weren't* rather than who they *were*.

People always ate in their categories.

This was the sign to everyone of which category you were in. If you ate with tax collectors, you were a tax collector. If you ate with rabbis, you were most likely a rabbi. If you were a rabbi and ate with a tax collector, you were stooping down to their level, thus lowering yourself. This was viewed as heresy. Ultimately, it was this that got Jesus killed. Jesus was a rabbi who ate with tax collectors and "sinners." Someone from the top category eating with those in the bottom. What Jesus did was so socially unacceptable, it angered many at the top enough to make them want to put him to death. But eating below his "category" was one way in which Jesus dealt with the human condition.

I was at the airport waiting to fly somewhere. And I noticed there were two lines of people waiting to board the plane. The first line, where most of the people were. And the second line, with businessmen and a special red carpet. This was the *exclusive* line. This little old lady walked up and tried to walk the red carpet, but the woman taking the tickets told her she was in the wrong line. After snapping at her, the old lady had to go to the back. We are still doing the category thing. In high school, the drama nerds like myself all sat at one table and all the jocks at another. The category thing. And if you messed with the social normalcy, you couldn't be in any category.

Jesus refused to only love those in his category.[1] Christians too often imagine that if there are two lines to heaven, they are always in the red-carpeted one. That they are always at the right table. Paul says there is only one line. And *everyone* is in it. That we are all broken sinners. Americans with their civil religion believe they are in the right line and that God is in our line with us. Someone told me they overheard Billy Graham say that if God doesn't judge America, he may have to apologize to Sodom and Gomorrah.

The original sin of America is that we have deified arrogance and

---

1. This idea is developed throughout *Gracism: The Art of Inclusion* by David A. Anderson (InterVarsity Press, 2007).

think that there are two lines and that we are in the right one. Real love doesn't respect the categories. It will embrace those in the other categories in order to become redemption.

Mario the Prophet

Religion is often the place where we most encounter sin and the powers of evil.

For instance, look at the first time Jesus casts out a demon. In the gospel of Mark, on the Sabbath, the day the Jews would gather for worship, a man came forward with an evil spirit. Jesus looks at the young man and speaks to the demon and tells the demon he should go somewhere else or the demon will be in trouble. After having a short but clever conversation with the demon that had manifested itself, Jesus tells the demon to be quiet. What's surprising about this story is *where* it happened. Now, it would have been one thing had it been in some dark alleyway behind a Walmart with people selling drugs, and Jesus calls out the demon and converts some pimp or something. That would have made sense. It would have been one thing had it been in some mental institution, but it wasn't. Where did it happen? *It happened in a synagogue.* Let me put it another way. The first demon possession in the New Testament was at a religious event. That says something to me. My community does this thing before the sermon called the greeting time. I will get up and tell everyone to turn to a neighbor and say something corny like, "Say to your neighbor hello, and God thinks you are a butterfly." So we all turn, blindly and awkwardly, to whatever random neighbor God haphazardly put us next to, and exchange pleasantries. Then we sit down and forget the person's name. I like greeting time, don't get me wrong, but that's what normally happens.

What freaks me out is, at the end of the day, when Jesus encounters the evil in the world, it's not always in some dark alley with a pimp; often it's during greeting time. In the New Testament, *Jesus encountered evil in religion all the time.* Religion crucified Jesus. Religion denounced Jesus' purposes. And I think Jesus is dealing with the same stuff in the same places today. I don't know why, but for some odd reason we think that when we are at church we are safe from evil. Like church is a bubble of protection from the powers of darkness that are all over the place in the evil "out there."

A friend of mine, who worked at a really huge church down the street, said that every once in a while, when the ushers at his church would gather the offering baskets, they would find a sealed envelope that when opened was empty. That means someone was either forgetful or wanted to look like they were giving without actually having to give. The only people who would know would be those who opened the giving envelopes, counted the money, and recorded the deposit. That's messy, but that's the culture of much of our community. We have developed a community that celebrates the look of giving, but somewhere along the way we lost the point; our message has said we honor the look of giving over the heart of giving.

Jesus is still encountering that kind of stuff.

In the original Super Mario, the one with the Duck Hunt, there were these little ghosts that would come after you and try to kill you. When you looked at them, they would stop coming toward you. When you looked the other way and ignored them, they came closer. When we ignore evil, whatever it is, *we give it more power.* At church we don't look at the darkness, because we think it's "out there."

I think Mario would be mad. Probably Jesus, too.

Picking Up the Mat

Jesus solved the whole sin and darkness thing by coming to be in our category with us. And then, he saves us. But we must never forget where we came from. When we spend more time with Jesus, we start to think we have been in the right line this whole time. Maybe our problem is that we forget how screwed up we are after we have been hanging out with people who claimed to be healed all the time, and so we develop an acute case of holy-am-I-itis. We accommodate ourselves to the belief that, now that we are on Jesus' team, all is well and dirtiness has been swept away; I think that is partly true. But not entirely. I've noticed an anomaly in Jesus' ministry. Have you ever noticed that after showing up somewhere to heal someone in his Godlike bravado, he always commands the healed to pick up their mat and take it home with them? As if stumbling away all caddywampus from their new healing, walking upright wasn't enough. But for Jesus there is always an added, seemingly needless (and heavy) command.

Pick up your mat.

Take it with you.

I wonder if some of these ambulatory ex-blind thought Jesus was being sarcastic. Or just plain funny. You just healed me and you want me to go home to my cesspool-like existence all healed, with that nasty old mat I would otherwise throw away or just give to Goodwill? But you'd do it. 'Cause this guy healed you and apparently is more than a healing charlatan. He's more than that. So with new sight, new ability to walk, new life, you walk home carrying with you the very thing that represents the old you. Kind of funny, isn't it? In giving new life, Jesus asks us to carry home the thing that represents the old life. Imagine you are that guy. Healed. You can walk. What do you do now that your life has been handed back to you as a gift from heaven? You'd have parties. New friends over. And as the evening ends, your friends stand up to leave, use the toilet, put on their coats. But they stand confused, staring at what they see in the coat closet. There before them stands the dirtiest, ugliest mat anyone has ever seen. Just dangling there. You'd ask, wouldn't you? "What is *that*?" That's when the story of the old you gets told. I get scared that sometimes religious people leave their mat behind with Jesus. That they deny they ever had a mat. But Jesus says to take it with us. So we never forget. So we never pass beyond that. So we keep being dependent on Jesus.

A Catholic friend of mine once explained to me the purpose of that water you dip your finger into when you enter the church and make the sign of the cross. He told me it is supposed to represent you being baptized again. And how after a long week, we all need to be baptized into Jesus again. I like that idea. I always need new grace. Every day. That looks like taking my mat with me.

Hell

Hell is real. It sucks that God had to go there.

Sometimes God is portrayed with this cold, Spock-like seriousness, as though sin was the end of the world. Is sin really God's biggest problem? It isn't. God has bigger problems. Sin was already defeated. Sure, God hates sin. But I'm rather sure God hates sin the same way I hate dirty diapers. I'll always hate their diapers, but I'll never confuse the diaper with the baby. I remember one of these phrases I learned early on: "Love the sinner, hate the sin." Someone once told me this is like cuddling up to someone, putting our lips to their ears, and whispering "I love you" with really bad garlic breath. We've got that statement all wrong. It wasn't Jesus' method. It's supposed to go: "Love the sinner, love the sinner." Being a follower of Jesus and not loving the unlikeable is on par with eating a Big Mac while watching *The Biggest Loser.*

Christian spirituality goes wrong when we compare all the things we are good at with the world's sin. That's not *authentic.* And I rarely use the a-word. By and large I don't like the word *authentic.* It's overdone. Everyone talks about wanting to be it, but nobody really does it. If I am actually authentic with people, I'm pretty sure they wouldn't be my friend afterward. The word carries with it weight we don't intend to mean. For some, *authentic* means anything that isn't a big church. For others, it means they have a right to be a jerk. We worship the word. If we claim it, we can do anything. *I'm being authentic, which means I can be mean or be a jerk.* Now, even though it is overdone, we still need it. Here is something I have found entirely true. When we exist in *authentic* relationship, it makes our darkness and depravity rise to the surface. It's bound to happen. Perhaps no more challenging is protecting our hearts from comparing ourselves with others. Only children, like myself, are the worst at this, because we didn't have a childhood where we *weren't* the most important thing in the world to our parents. Having to live with others, in community, forces us to realize we are not the most important people in the world. Becoming a follower of Jesus fixed that in me. Because Christian faith requires you to believe there is a God. And if you follow Jesus, you quickly come to the realization that you aren't God's only child. This reality is a challenging one to grasp. Sin, therefore, translates itself into each of us, comparing our best with other people's worst. Or us comparing our worst with other people's best. At its worst, we become like Ross Perot, pulling out our tables and charts and PowerPoint presentations to prove to ourselves and everyone else how incredible we are in comparison to the rest of the world.

Sometimes I worry that we've made hell the place we think people who really annoy us go to.

That hell is a place for people in the other categories that we don't like or that make us uncomfortable. This was not Jesus' way of talking about hell. This used to really trip me up; I liked a God who never judged anyone. It presents a conundrum for us. As time has gone on, though, it's been incredulously challenging for me to believe in a guy who talked about hell so much. Not that I don't believe him. I just don't like the notion of hell. Then I noticed something. This one time I took a class on public speaking. The number one rule, it turns out, is to not only prepare something to say but prepare your understanding of *who* you are talking to. That is, your audience will say more than your own words. Look at Jesus and his discussion on hell. Jesus, yes, has a discernable sense of frustration toward the Pharisees and Sadducees; so he warns them of hell. But even more than that, Jesus clarifies to his disciples that they need to be worried about hell. "It is better to have one less eye than go to hell with your whole body."[2]

Jesus warns his own disciples about hell.

Why? I wonder if maybe Jesus uses the idea of hell to get his disciples to stop being so darn complacent. To stop thinking they are in the only category that God likes. Then I read this part of the Bible where it says that after Jesus dies, he goes to hell for a couple of days to preach love and mercy to those who were there. Compelling thought. Even God goes to hell in the Bible. And he does this to save people. In the most hopeless of categories. I kind of wonder how someone could read that and not see, through and through, the love of God on every side.

Hugs

Because it's all about those in the categories that make us uncomfortable. Chris was so cool. He was a barista at a coffee shop down the street from my house. He'd smoke on his break and read philosophy and make coffee for a living. Chris was the type of guy who'd go to political rallies for really fringe politicians, and not just the right- or left-wingers. He voted for politicians that didn't even have right or left anymore, but use colors. He only bought food at organic grocery stores, used tofu in everything from sandwiches to spaghetti, and thought people who drove Hummers were modern-day Nazis. And if you told him you shopped, he'd go off about how Walmart and the nuclear holocaust were of the same level of immorality. He read a lot. He'd see me reading too, and we'd talk about what we were thinking. I'd listen to his crazy twenty-eight-year-old theories on how capitalism and the American dream were destroying the earth. I'd talk about Kierkegaard and existentialism and how mad I was that certain politicians monopolized Jesus.

We became friends quickly. Small talk became medium talk.

---

2. Matthew 5:29 paraphrased.

Medium talk became big talk. And one thing led to another. Taking things to second base, we thought we'd get a burger one night. We went to this joint called McMennamins at midnight. We met up in the dark corner in the back room. We told stories, shared theories, and laughed. He wasn't a Christian, but his parents were, which made for some laughs. He knew I was a Christian and was fine with it. We never really got into anything too deep about faith. Early in the morning, our burgers were done and we were about to leave, and he looks at me and out of nowhere asks me a question.

"What do you think about gay people?"

I was entirely caught off guard. That week our state was voting on a gay-rights thing, and everyone and their dog was talking about it. But the way he asked was kind of funny. It felt weird; I didn't know why. But I get asked that a lot, by a lot of people. It's a really hard thing for many Christians to talk about. They don't know what to say. At the same time, I know everything the Bible says about homosexuality. At least to the best of my ability to know, Jesus never even touched on the subject. So with my experience and what I know about what the Scriptures say, I have really struggled with this. Caught in the middle. It's hard. All of this, and I'm sitting in front of a guy who is not a Christian, who knows I am one and that I pastor a bunch of them, and he is asking me what I think about gay people. So I told him what I normally say and told him some of the things the Bible says, but then I asked him a question.

"What do you think, Chris?"

The second I said that, his head went down into his lap. I could tell something I had said had pricked something inside of him. Either he didn't want to answer my question, or I had completely hurt his feelings; for some odd reason he couldn't answer. But he did. And his answer would change me for the rest of my life.

He said, "I can't answer that. I didn't know how to tell you, *but I'm gay.*"

I had no idea. My mind heard those words over and over and over like a broken record. I was speechless. But I also knew at that very moment, with our eyes locked and the moment holy, I had to do something. So I did. I did all I could do. If God no longer has a ten-foot pole, why should I? And to this moment I think it was all Jesus would let me do. I stood up and told him to stand up too. He did, but looked kind of confused. I put my arms out, around his upper body, pulled him close to mine, *and hugged him*. After realizing I wasn't trying to kiss him, he put his arms around me and we hugged. For like a minute, too. People around us chuckled. Then I let go, looked him in the eyes, and said, "I love you." That was all I could do. And I am convinced at that moment I became a Christian for one of the first times in my life. Right there in a bar. And I say that because becoming a Christian for me has become less and less about canned prayers and more about opportunities that God gives you to love and hug. That night I became a Christian all over again. And today, we are still friends.

And when I see him, I still hug him.

CHAPTER

Why We Don't Laugh: Messy Sex

SIX

Sex is paradoxical. The poet Thomas Lynch says we're all dying for it, and because of it.[1] Let's talk about why that might be.

Sex Ed

It's nearly impossible to forget the good ole days when we'd fall to the ground in a swarm of violent hilarity every time someone uttered the word *sex*. Remember that? Nothing topped it. It was insatiable. No matter the seriousness of the kid, how smart they were, their upbringing, if they were in TAG or not, what cereal they ate; something about

---

1. Thomas Pynch quoted in Lynch, *Bodies in Motion and at Rest*, 25. If you haven't already, buy Pynch's entire collection and read it over a Christmas break.

the word made us all go nuts. Language, race, or school didn't make a lick of difference; *sex* was like this universal inside joke that all twelve-year-olds couldn't keep from snickering at wherever and whenever they encountered it. Even if our third-grade teacher uttered the word in the context of some in-class conversation about biology or human anatomy, we just couldn't control ourselves. Like trying to hold in a sneeze.

Sex ed was almost certainly my favorite class ever. It was basically comedy hour, wasn't it? Over and over they'd speak the word, and there we'd be waiting for the class to get over so we could all go out in the hall afterward and laugh till the end of the day. Especially where I was schooled. The first name of the poor individual who had the dastardly responsibility of teaching sex ed at our elementary school was actually Ed. No joke. It took years of heartfelt reflection to figure out that Sex Ed was not his *actual* name. When I found out it wasn't, I felt really stupid. But I didn't know. He, Sex Ed, would walk into class and I'd get really uncomfortable inside. I'd imagine, who has sex in his name? Why do they call him that? *He must have problems.* We'd watch grainy instructional videos on birthing and STDs and then we learned how to put a condom on a banana. Because these are the things that sex is all about at that stage in life. Birthing, STDs, and safe bananas.

This idea of sex was so mysterious to all of us back then. We thought you could accidently impregnate a girl just by looking at her long enough. Or that you needed protection for making out. I didn't know. None of us did. There were always a few kids at the time who claimed they'd gone to second or third base or something like that. This only made sense to those of us who got baseball. Baseball metaphors, sadly, didn't make sense to many in this regard. We were still talking about the word *sex*. No matter our place in life, at its very utterance, we'd look at each other and snicker like we were in on this epic and primal inside joke. Oh, how this foreign word had power over us. It captured us like a bear trap. But it obviously was an indescribable power that grown-ups seemed to have missed out on. They'd look at us, almost embarrassingly, as though we were stupid or immature for finding such joy in the small things of life. *Maybe they didn't get it.* The word clearly didn't seem to have the same power on them as it did on us. But when we all get older, we look back on ourselves in hindsight and realize our joy was the most irrational form of joy in the world.

Why would we laugh? *Sex* isn't necessarily a funny word. There's nothing inherently comical about it. I'd have a hard time believing that if Jerry Seinfeld climbed up on stage and just said the word over and over, that any of us would laugh. We'd start throwing things. Or demand refunds. But back then, the most boring of teachers could say it in a lecture on Shakespeare and they had us rolling. Weird. Because apparently the older we get, the less sex is funny.

My theory on sex is, the more we've had it or think we understand everything about it, *the less mysterious it becomes.* And we stop laughing. It becomes, well, controlled.

It was my fifteenth year of life when I first saw a girl naked. In the school's murky locker room, a friend opened his zip-up backpack to grab, not a pair of Nikes for gym class, but a small shiny magazine. He opened this little magazine. The pictures looked different. They were shiny. Perfect. Fleshy. Like a little boy stumbling into the closet in Narnia, that little glossy magazine effectively took me from a world of innocence to a world of the grown-ups. These pictures were glossy like none I'd seen before. And they had perfect and pretty people in it. And they were naked. Together. I'll never forget that moment. You probably haven't either. From that moment, we all enter a new world. A world that Scotty can never beam you out of.

My friend Nate told me about this moment for him. He said that he can't remember his first-grade teacher's name, but he can still remember the first time he saw the glossy perfect people in the magazine. It was *that* impactful. That moment, especially for dudes, is very memorable. It's simply burned into our male brains.

Since that moment, for many, it seems as though we chase a mirage that simply doesn't exist. Striving. Hiking. Looking. Searching. For something that lives in our imagination. Ideal sexuality. We all are looking for something that doesn't exist. At least not where we're looking. Because the idea of sex that most of us have been sold doesn't exist. Anywhere. Oddly enough, though, I believe in searching for that mirage we stumble upon ourselves. There in the mirror, we are forced to ask a greater question: Who made me like this? Why do I search for this? There's a very important reason.

In Christian spirituality, authentic sexuality and redemption are Siamese twins.

Mystery

It's been a long time since I've laughed at the word. Not sure exactly why. Saying it to myself now just doesn't conjure up the laughter of days gone by. Not to mention it just feels plain silly saying the word to myself. But the mysteriousness of it lives on.

When we stop laughing, we stop wondering.[2] It's like someone has died. Someone inside; this little odd and somewhat perverse child that unwittingly took joy in life's small things is silenced forever. It's now gone. Then other kids stopped laughing at it too. When did it become so serious? From then on out, we became like the grown-ups. Looking at kids with disgust when they chuckled at the word, like *they* were the immature ones. *They* were dumb. *They* were uninformed. Hence, a new me, the grown-up me, was born. Maybe we stop laughing when it becomes so commonplace. When it becomes a normal part of life. When everyone starts doing it. When it becomes commodified and commercialized and marketed. It's no longer funny; it becomes a way

---

2. Wondering is very important to the life of faith. See the classic Jewish theologian Abraham Joshua Heschel, *I Asked for Wonder: A Spiritual Anthology*, ed. Samuel H. Dresner (Crossroad, 1983).

of life. It's serious business now. It's not funny. Because we think we understand it completely now. Once it's rationalized, it no longer breathes mystery to us.

We should all laugh uncontrollably when we hear the word *God*.

There's this story of a community of First Nation Native American Hopi people who originally lived in present-day Arizona. These desert-dwelling people sang songs around the fire like any other people group. To this day, what's interesting is what most of their music is about. If you'd listen to the songs the Hopi sing, invariably their singing always goes back to one thing. *Rain*. Which, in the desert, is hard to come by. It's interesting, isn't it? The very thing they sing the most about is the one thing they have very little of. *Rain*.[3]

Is this why we sing so much about sex? And love?

It's interesting, isn't it, that we live at a time in history when people are having more sex than ever before, yet are singing so much more about love? Is it maybe because we have confused the two? Maybe if we were full of love we would sing songs about other things. Like beauty. And truth. And justice.

Cardboard Signs

As Jesus nears Jericho on his final journey to Jerusalem, he stops to converse with a man holding a cardboard sign. This is going to be his last miracle before dying. The man with the cardboard sign is called Bartimaeus; you may know him as Blind Bartimaeus. He sits there, day by day, blind as a bat. Waiting. Hearing Jesus is coming by, he stands to his feet. After yelling at Jesus for mercy, the man with the cardboard sign hears Jesus call his name. He comes and leaves his cardboard sign behind. Jesus gives him sight. Then the story says Jesus keeps going on his way to Jerusalem to face his pending death. And

---

3. This story is inspired by Leonard Sweet, *The Three Hardest Words in the World to Get Right* (Colorado Springs: Waterbrook, 2006), 95.

right behind is his new friend Bartimaeus. With his new eyes and no cardboard sign.[4]

It's an interesting story, because Jesus gave Bartimaeus sight so he could use his new eyes *to see Jesus die*. It is imperative that we understand the method with which Jesus heals. He does it not just so Bartimaeus is healed, but so he can follow and see him die. And then rise. When he heals part of Bartimaeus, it's so Bartimaeus can see a new part of Jesus.

We are Bartimaeus with cardboard signs. When we are fully healed people, we will fully see him. Sadly, this just won't happen this side of eternity. But when we are sexually healed, we see God a little more. Like Bartimaeus, who had a cardboard sign. A sign with his deep human needs written all over it. His blindness. Because we all write on our signs the thing we all yearn and crave to be healed from.

America's cardboard sign has the word *sex* written on it.

America has done to sex what the Israelites did to the golden calf. We've worshiped it. It seems to me that American Christianity, carrying its own burden of guilt, has done to the church what pornography has done to our culture. It has made *everything* about size. This is why pastors' conferences are so darn hard for me. On one level, it's mostly hard to go to pastors' conferences because I'm under thirty and I don't wear leather bracelets or have floppy hair in the front; although I do sport a pair of the dark-rimmed glasses. Also, they don't put pastors of little churches like me on the stage, and for good reason. Most of us don't have anything special to say or what others want to hear. But every year, I go to one conference with my friend Ryan who started a church in Portland and owns a pub. I like Ryan. He keeps me laughing, like Quinn did in Bible college.

---

4. This story is found in Mark 10:46–52. I of course take liberties in replacing the "cloak" of Bartimaeus with a cardboard sign. It makes more sense for us.

We both struggle with conferences because people will always ask us how big the churches are that we serve.

It wouldn't be an inordinately challenging thing to answer. Depending on the Sunday, we can both gauge how many people are in the pews with a couple of hands. It's the nature of the question that I can't stand. Because what we're really asking each other when we get together isn't about the size of our church. Really, what we're doing is sizing each other up so we can feel more comfortable around each other. When we ask each other how big *our* church is, we might as well just say what we're all really thinking. *Do I up you or do you up me?*

It's almost certain that Jesus would not be asked to speak at our pastors' conferences, because the community he had gathered numbered about twelve, one of which would deny him three times, and another who would sell him to be crucified. Jesus never worshipped numbers.

One person healed is the stuff that gets Jesus out of bed in the morning. One healed person. Holistic Jesus spirituality seeks to heal the *whole* of the human person, not just the little parts.[5] Not the spiritual dimension alone. Not the physical side only. *Everything.* Oddly, some forms of the gospel have been purported as simply being about saving souls to go to heaven. In this paradigm, our Jesus du jour only cares about populating heaven, something Jesus undeniably cares deeply about. Yet the Jesus of his day did more than just talk about going to heaven. It is only half of the story of Jesus' purposes. Jesus came to save every side of the human person. God knows we are all multidimensional people with different sides to each of us. Knowing and healing all sides is essential to returning us to a healed picture of God's *imago Dei*—God's image in each of us. Jesus had many sides to his life. So do we.

---

5. Eugene H. Peterson, *Five Smooth Stones for Pastoral Work* (1980; Grand Rapids: Eerdmans, 1992), 29.

Ever wonder why we have four gospels to tell the same story about the same person? Either God has a real problem with repeating himself, or there is a reason for having *four gospels*: Matthew, Mark, Luke, and John. For instance, Mark, a secretary for Peter, tells us the story of Jesus for a Gentile community, most likely in Rome. Luke, a doctor who traveled with Paul and who most likely didn't know Jesus personally, tells us the story of Jesus from the perspective of a physician who gives way too many details. Matthew, a true Jew of the Jews, recounts the story of Jesus from the perspective of the Christ who is the fulfillment of the Jewish Scriptures and anticipations. And finally, John, the mystic, offers us the story of Jesus kind of like a poet sitting in the back of the coffee shop who gives us the story of the mysterious Jesus. But why did the authors of the New Testament and the early church decide we needed more than one side of the Jesus story? Why not just one story? Because Jesus, incarnate God, has many sides to him.

Philosophers call this a parallax.[6] It is when we choose to look at the same object from different angles to see it in different lights. When we do this, it becomes new again. Neither God nor a human can be understood from just one side.

Maybe we're like Jesus in that one point of view just isn't good enough. Maybe when you're looking at something as majestic as the Savior of the world—Jesus—more than one documentary is necessary. He's just that darn incredible. Maybe looking at Jesus from one angle isn't safe; not just unsafe, but unorthodox. Because to *really see* Jesus, we need more than one set of eyes. We need four people to tell one story. The human person is incredible in their own way. I can't *fix* anyone, because only God sees all the sides. I only see one. You can't fix me, because you only see one side. This is why the Bible says we are fearfully

---

6. This idea of parallax is inspired by Slavoj Žižek, *The Parallax View*, Short Circuits (Cambridge, MA: MIT Press, 2006). Žižek is a ridiculously challenging author to engage, but he is beyond smart. If you get the chance, try out one of his books.

and wonderfully made. The whole creation is. It all screams about its maker.

The mystic writer Meister Eckhart once said that every creature is a word of God and a book about God. That is, humans scream God. The rabbis who studied the book of Genesis in the Torah believed that God had made twenty-six universes before this one.[7] After twenty-six tries, this one simply turned out to be the best, the most perfected.[8] That implies humans as we know them today have gone through many test runs.

There are sides to us that just one person can't tell. Sides that are visible and sides that are hidden. We all have many sides. We each have an emotional side. A spiritual side. A sexual side. And to get the whole story with holistic healing, we need to see all pictures together. Every side must be healed. In order for our spiritual side to be healed, we must be willing to be healed emotionally. In order for our sexual side to be healed, we must be willing to be healed spiritually.

Because Jesus can't heal just one side. It's not in his nature.

Jesus Up in Our Grill

Jesus brings sexual healing to those who are open to it. St. Augustine said it best: "God made us without our permission *but will not save us without our consent*."[9] We have to be open to being healed and saved.

There's an incredible young woman whom I live with in community who has struggled with her sexual identity for years. In college, she was

---

7. This and other important themes in Jewish understandings of the creation of the world are found in Adin Steinsaltz, *Biblical Images*, enl. ed., trans. Yehuda Hanegbi and Yehudit Keshet (1984; Northvale, NJ: Jason Aronson, 1994).

8. Charles Cummings, *Eco-Spirituality: Toward a Reverent Life* (Mahwah, NJ: Paulist Press, 1991), 30.

9. St. Augustine quoted in John Amsberry, *More of You Through Prayer* (Bloomington, IN: AuthorHouse, 2009), 5 (emphasis mine).

out as a lesbian. Now, as a Christian, she has told me on a number of occasions how she has prayed fervently for God to heal her and bring her to a real understanding of who she is. Another friend of mine used to be in the pornography business and is learning that she is not simply her ability to put out for the camera. Another couple is learning how to have a healthy sexuality after years of sexual and emotional abuse. Jesus initiates sexual healing to all who are willing.

Thomas Schmidt talks about how the power of the gospel is not about looking down on others' sexual sin on a television screen but about looking at sexual sin in the mirror.[10] That is, when we encounter Christ, we invariably encounter our own sexuality at the deepest of levels.

Another story of Jesus' healing power is in the gospel of John, when Jesus encounters a woman by a well who had been married a number of times. In the span of a couple of minutes of discussion about the weather, Jesus asks her where her husband is—insinuating that the one she is sleeping with at the time is one of a long line of lovers. She has been with eight people. All of this in a couple of lines of conversation. Now let's pause for a moment from the awkward tension of this conversation. Does it surprise you *how quickly Jesus gets into this woman's sex life*? It takes a few minutes of conversation before they are on to the sex thing. Jesus, not known for small talk or platitudes, digs right in. She blushed, I'm sure.

What surprises me about being a Christian for a number of years isn't that Jesus fixes us right away; *it's how insatiably fast he's willing to get into our sex lives.* Let me put it another way. I don't know one person of the Christian spiritual tradition whom I'm close to that is not wrestling with their sexuality on some level. Do you? And how quickly he gets involved with all of us. When we encounter Christ, in

---

10. Thomas E. Schmidt, *Straight and Narrow? Compassion and Clarity in the Homosexuality Debate* (Downers Grove, IL: InterVarsity Press, 1995), 55.

his healing power, our sexuality is *always* being engaged. Because our sexuality is so close to who we are as people. As God's people. To be sexual is to be in covenant—committed relationship. In the overarching narrative of the Scriptures, sex and marriage go hand in hand. And to be sexually intimate is to be married. Scot McKnight says there is no such thing in the Bible as premarital sex.[11] I agree. Because when a man and a woman are in a sexual relationship—they're married.

Sex Change

Jesus is wrestling with all of us on this stuff. Yet in its history, the Christian church has always wrestled with itself on the topic of sexuality. For a number of reasons. We have a rather tattered past regarding the issue.

St. Augustine believed that sin, the power of evil, was *literally* passed on through semen. Pope Leo IX signed a rule in the tenth century saying that those in the priesthood could not masturbate.[12] Many of the early church fathers castrated themselves on the basis that they could otherwise not have served Jesus. In fact, I would argue that to the degree that our understanding of God is healed, our sexuality will be healed. For instance, the very issue of God's "gender" is tearing the church apart. Is God really a man? There are images in the Bible of God being a man, for sure. But does that literally mean he has a penis? Jesus was a man, for sure. No question there. Frankly, any question about Spirit is a hard question to answer, because any astute student of the Scriptures and history will notice that Spirit has undergone, simply put, a bit of change and process.

The first time Spirit was talked about in the Hebrew tradition, it was called *Ruach*, which in Hebrew is a feminine noun. Then when the

---

11. Scot McKnight, *The Blue Parakeet: Rethinking How You Read the Bible* (Grand Rapids: Zondervan, 2008), 118.
12. Pope Leo IX quoted in Mel White, *Stranger at the Gate: To Be Gay and Christian in America* (1994; New York: Penguin, 1995), 16.

Greeks came along, in the New Testament they called it *Pneuma*, which is a neuter noun. Then the Latins came. Oh, the Latins. They called it *Spiritus*, which is a masculine noun. And this was done, it seems, because at least some religious folk for centuries have been doing the very best they can to ensure that all the members of the Trinity are as male as possible. The problem with that is that it's too tidy; it cleans up the mess where we ought to leave the mystery.

I refer to God as "he" for a number of reasons. But this doesn't mean that I think God is constricted by our two human, biological sexes. In essence God is neither a man nor a woman, but spirit.[13] This is one reason why we must guard against making God in our own image, whether in our thoughts or our language, for just the reverse is the truth we need to embrace.[14] Ultimately, humanity has done to God's Spirit what we've done to ourselves. The Spirit, over a couple of thousand years, has gone through a bit of a "sex change." That's a long sex change. I don't like that. God's Spirit was never intended to be defined by its genitalia (or lack thereof). So we don't always know what to do with this she/it/he. And we don't know what to do with ourselves either.

I tell my theology students that the Word will always transcend our words. It is one thing to use words to talk about the Creator and quite another to use them to talk about the creature. Yet we still believe in words and use them. For us, language relates directly to being made in God's image and likeness. But God is always bigger than words. It's hard for us, maybe, but we've got to let God be God, and we've got to let ourselves be what he made us. If we can't accept God for who God is, we can't accept ourselves for who we are.

But there is beauty in the Christian understanding of sex. The early church fathers spoke of the *"aversio a Deo per conversionem ad creaturam"*—the human condition called sin is all about turning

---

13. Numbers 23:19; John 4:24.
14. Deuteronomy 4:15–16; Genesis 1:26–27.

away from the Creator to creation for our fulfillment. We turn from covenant to coveting. From relationship to restless unsatisfaction. This means, in the right context, sexuality is God's glory. It is wonderful. And beautiful. As long as it doesn't become about the sex. As long as it remains holy. To God. One biblical scholar argues that every sexual sin in the Bible is in reference to the breakdown of this covenant.[15]

An entire book of the Bible is about naked people depicting a love scene between a man and a woman in covenant. It is called the Song of Solomon and it's about God's love for his people. Sexuality outside the context of covenant is *always* destructive. When it doesn't take into account the rest of the human person and their history—it hurts. The lure of pornography is sexuality free from the messiness of humanity. It doesn't take into account the *real* things of life. Disagreement. Argument. Struggle. *Authentic humanity.* Pornography never has a section at the end showing how the relationship has continued after the act of sexuality. It's all about the sex only. I think what porn does to the people involved is worse. It tells them that their worth is what they can do on this video for this amount of money. That is the epitome of hell if you ask me. When my value is that. Or your value is that.

Baptisms Again

There were different kinds of people who claimed to be Christians after Jesus. Some thought Jesus wasn't God. Others that he was only God and not human. Still others that he was some nicer form of the really mad God from the Old Testament. It's entirely imaginable why these sorts of groups had widespread appeal. Maybe I would have joined one. Or started one. I don't know. But many of these groups were deemed wrong. Some call them heretical. And for good reason. Lots of them were dangerous; on various fronts. So from day one there were all of these internal struggles regarding the nature of God and Christ.

---

15. Schmidt, *Straight and Narrow?*, 53.

The primitive Christians also had a number of reputations. Unlike today, being normal wasn't one of them. First-century philosophers and thinkers were rather suspicious that these Christians—whose "all-powerful" leader had been crucified—were sort of atheists who didn't believe in the gods. This was believed about them because they were unwilling to worship the golden idols everyone so faddishly worshipped. *You couldn't see their God.* Because, for this community, the God of the universe didn't fit on the dinner table and certainly outdid any idol.

On a popular level, the general public was rather suspicious that these communities were baby eaters, and for good reason. They would celebrate something called the *agape* feast, or the "love feast." We call it communion. Communion, in the end, turned out to be bad marketing for the early church, because everyone thought Christians were cannibals. Hard to market with *that* perception. What would you think if you had a friend who joined a cult that celebrated a weekly meal called the *agape feast*, claiming to memorialize a dead thirty-three-year-old carpenter executed by the puppet government alongside two other criminals crucified for armed robbery? You'd freak. They'd insist: "We don't eat babies. Just to clarify, we do *pretend to eat thirty-three-year-old dead carpenters, though.* But please, don't confuse the two. We swear we don't eat babies." Truth be told, Christians have always been embarrassed cannibals. What are we supposed to say? We eat Jesus. And drink his blood. Think about it. What other religion starts the week by talking about eating a dead criminal? Look at their name, too. Early on, the only name they called themselves was "the way." In terms of a name, we only really know of two of them, although they may have had more. Apparently, somebody gave them a nickname: they called them *christianoi.*[16] That is, "little Christs." But this was most likely not the kindest term of endearment. Most think it was an insult of sorts. A

---

16. Acts 11:25–26.

kind of "Ohhh . . . look at you. So cute, little Christ-man." This is what they were *called*. They *called themselves* "the way." Of the two, one stuck and is used today. The insult stuck.

It's interesting to me that the insult stuck. Back then, to be a Christian literally meant to wear an insult on your sleeve. Over time, the name became an honor. Baptisms made for an interesting story too.

What made Christians overwhelmingly unique was their baptism. It's believed by historians that the earliest Christians, when they were baptized, weren't marched into the waters with a white robe like today. And thank God. If you've ever seen a little girl get baptized with one of these church robes on, she looks like she might drown every time. Back then, they didn't have the budget for the robes yet. Or a market for them. So in front of whoever was there, often their family, they would get carried down to the water and get immersed in the waters of death. And they would be baptized *completely naked*. They would literally take off their clothes where they were and get baptized naked. Right where they were. (St. Francis maybe heard about this.) And this wasn't because the early church had a thing for weird baptisms. And when they were done, after taking off their old clothes, they would arise from the water, go to the shore, and put on a *new pair of clothes*.[17]

When they did this, it was like they were saying that all of us are back at the garden. We are new again. In Christ there is no shame. Paul would even tell a couple of churches to clothe yourself with Christ Jesus.

When you are in Jesus, nakedness is no longer your shame. Christ becomes your shame. And you can simply wear that shame on your back.

---

17. On this whole naked baptism thing, see chapter 1, "The Garments of Shame," in Jonathan Z. Smith, *Map Is Not Territory: Studies in the History of Religions* (Leiden: E. J. Brill, 1978; Chicago: University of Chicago Press, 1993).

A Naked Wife

Nakedness, in the context of covenant, is God embodying love of the broken. This prophet by the name of Hosea in the Old Testament was told by God that he was to go and find a prostitute and marry her. Take her as his wife. This was to be a sign to the people of Israel, who had whored themselves out to other gods, that God was still into them. So Hosea went and found himself a prostitute. That conversation would have been interesting.

"Hi, thirty shekels for the night."

"I'm not here for the sex."

"What are you here for?"

"You."

"Are you a cop?"

"No."

"What are you?"

"A prophet from God."

I think it would have made Christmas parties with all the other prophets interesting. Wouldn't it? "Well, Hosea, great to see you. Who is this?"

We call this an *enacted* prophecy.

It was a prophecy put to action. There were other prophecies like this. In the book of Ezekiel, God tells the prophet to lie down on his side for the number of days the people would be in captivity. In Jeremiah, God has him walk around with no shoes on to preach to the people in sin. St. Francis of Assisi did this. He apparently, after a childhood of wealth, sold it all and literally ran through the streets of the well-to-do Assisi naked to preach. Because sometimes prophecies deserve to be acted out. Hosea married a prostitute. Because that is what God is like. It is like the holiest in the world taking into his room a complete whore.

That's a fascinating way to destroy evil in the world, isn't it? To marry it.

Only this God could destroy evil by marrying it. That's what God does to us. He marries us. Naked. Just as we are. Not as we're not. When I was a brand new Christian, someone told me I should write out a short list of the qualities of the person I wanted to marry. Perfect this. Perfect that. My list was long. I kept it in my pocket. It was my Perfect list. It strikes me as odd that when God chooses to write out a list of the qualities of his future wife, it has one word on it. *Whore.* We write out the same list of the people we choose to love. We love them when they have this or that—the things on our list. Jesus apparently had no list. Or he did and it had words like *whore* and *broken* and *imperfect* on it. There's this Bible called *Jesus Loves Porn Stars.* Some Christians think that is bad. But I wonder if they have ever read the book of Hosea.

For a couple of years it seemed really healthy for me to see a counselor. His name was Dale. He would ask me about my week, he would dig into my emotions—the stuff counselors do. He seemed to believe that pretty much all of my problems came from an incomplete relationship with my father. He was right in many ways. We would talk about sexuality. He was a Christian, which worried me, because I always thought maybe he would try to tell me how evil and bad sex was. He didn't. Dale told me how important sex is for our life. How central it is to being a human being—*and how!*—no matter our desire to escape from it; our lives have a ton to do with sex. One day Dale told me about the basement. He told me everyone in some way, shape, or form is secretly ashamed of their sexuality. How they hide things because they don't want anyone to know. It's that door off the kitchen. We all have rooms in our houses. The living room we keep meticulously clean so visitors are duped into thinking we actually clean the house. The bathrooms are clean for the same reason. Our bedrooms we keep nice just in case we have to go up there. Dale told me we keep things clean for an image. But there is always that door off the kitchen. You never take guests through it. It leads to someplace dark and dirty and full of things you hate about your life. We open it up and just throw crap down there. Eventually, we throw so much junk down there that it overflows, and it starts getting in our kitchen. Dale took me down to my basement. He said that health, the kind Jesus brings, is the kind that goes down to the basement and brings stuff out and talks about it. Asks things about it. *Why did I throw this down there? Why is this here?* If we start bringing stuff out of the basement, we start to see why we are so messed up. Too many of my friends don't have anyone to go into the basement with. I tell them Jesus will. He isn't scared of the basement.

The church is an *enacted* prophesy. We do this when we choose to admit, as followers of Christ, that we actually have basements. When we admit our vulnerability. When we admit our promiscuousness. When we don't put on spiritual makeup; when we're willing to try being naked in the presence of God.

And when the world sees we have a God who's *actually* willing to go into our basement with us and not get freaked out, maybe they'll let him come in too.

CHAPTER SEVEN

Botox Religion: Messy Relationships

Just recently, while chatting over lunch about culture, God, Christianity, and why America is impregnated with the heresy of individualism, a friend leaned in from his steamy fajitas and whispered a prophetic utterance under his garlicky breath. He was saying how America is the only country that came into existence by explorers who were *on their way to go somewhere else.* None of them wanted to be here. And how this might be why we, as Americans, are never happy where we are. Why we always try to be somewhere else. Then he observed that America is all about the "*i.*" We have iPods. We have iTunes. We have iPads. He said we can't even do the Wii without two *i*'s.[1]

---

1. Len Sweet told me this over lunch. I laughed out loud.

Truth be told, in my younger days I used to believe individualism had an overwhelming number of inherent benefits. Individualism claims that there is no compelling need to mess with people and their problems, that your problems are your only problems, and that everyone else can fend for themselves. But at the end of the day, I disagree with my old self.

With all its apparent benefits, it's almost certain that individualism and idolatry are relatives deeply interrelated. Wherever you find one, you'll most likely find the other.

Charlton Heston

Look at the ways we paint God. At this museum in the heart of London, I noticed that most of the paintings that portray God in heaven show him with this Americanesque Charlton Heston white beard, covered in Roman military garb, pointing down with his really big finger at the earth, this indignant look on his face like the world's in for it. If it isn't clear, just look at the bulging vein in his neck. It's rather difficult being a Christian looking at these kinds of paintings. Frankly, they're a little embarrassing. They make us want to whisper to the guy standing next to us with his fancy new camera, that the guy in the picture isn't as bad as he looks. He's not that mean. And he's probably not that white either; nor does he look like Charlton Heston. He looks too much like us, doesn't he? If I could, I'd probably tell him that God's more like the old creepy guy from the first *Home Alone*; he's not a dingy old murderous junky who picks through your garbage and is planning on killing you. After you get to know this weird old dude, when the movie has progressed, he's way friendlier than he looks. God, in reality, is always different than our paintings. There is an inherent danger in all of our paintings of God. They don't match up.[2] But humans, in their

---

2. Henry J. Cadbury, *The Peril of Modernizing Jesus* (1937; London: SPCK, 1962).

reality, are always convinced that a picture of themselves is the same as their God. But God is not like us. I promise.

When people who don't consider themselves of the Christian faith hear the way Christians talk about God, it would seem they have the opposite response. *Your God sounds nice, but in the end, he also sounds really judgmental.* My two hands couldn't count the number of times I've heard someone confess they'd never believe in a God that could invent a place like hell. Which brings me to a point. That in the context of our weird religious culture, everyone seems to have significant problems with the God they don't follow, and yet nobody seems to confess any problems with the God they do follow. By and large, the few and the brave are willing to share that they have problems *with the God they do follow.* The disciples had problems with Jesus, didn't they? Why can't we? True love for God must be marked not by total agreement but total fidelity *despite disagreement.* Like marriage. I used to have a beef with Jesus when he essentially said *I AM the great I AM* because it sounded so American.[3] So individualistic. So me-centered. Of course, that's not what Jesus meant at all. Because Jesus isn't individualistic. Or an American. He's part of the Trinity. But individualism as we know it has hijacked what Jesus said and laminated it as its vision statement. The individualistic individual confesses boldly: *I AM the great I AM.* Self-sufficient, omnipresent, and macho.

Today we desperately need a God that's not so like us. For to have a God that looks just like us is what the wise ones in the Old Testament

---

3. In the Old Testament, when God appears to Moses in the burning bush and recruits him for the job of leading the Israelites out of their slavery in Egypt, he tells him, "I AM WHO I AM. This is what you are to say to the Israelites: 'I AM has sent me to you'" (Exod. 3:14). Then in the New Testament, Jesus gets into a heated discussion with the Jews about who he is and being sent by God and all when he says to them, "I tell you the truth, ... before Abraham was born, I am!" (John 8:58). That would have got him killed if he hadn't slipped away.

call idols. Or iDolls. We all have one. A picture, a doll, an image of our perception of God that *always* looks a little too much like us. The trick is how to destroy the iDoll. And in the Scriptures, only one thing can do this. Rule number one: be suspicious of any god that claims to *look* just like we do and *approves* of everything we do.

One of my writing heroes, Anne Lamott, once overheard someone say that you know you've created God in your own image when God hates everyone that you hate.

The endgame is that we ultimately become the pictures of God, the idols, we construct. I wonder if we have pictures of a God who is all by himself up in heaven and is all judgy because we all live by ourselves on earth and are all judgy. The picture becomes our lived reality. Maybe if we pictured a God of three persons (Father, Son, Spirit) living in endless communal love with each other, welcoming all to God's grace, we would live together in endless communal love with each other and welcome all to God's grace. Scary as it is, God will inevitably look like us unless we go out of our way to destroy that iDoll. The world of individualism we inhabit today most needs a God that is not like it. It needs a God that is not *all* about the individual. This is fulfilled by the very one who invented the world in the Bible. For the one who actually invented the world is anything *but* individual. God, in God's nature, is a community. Creation was a group project, not a sole proprietorship. God is a board, not a CEO. If the Trinity is how we are supposed to live, we have something to learn.[4] One who calls himself the great I AM

---

4. For a theological basis of this, see Donald L. Gelpi, *The Divine Mother: A Trinitarian Theology of the Holy Spirit* (University Press of America, 1984); Colin E. Gunton, *The One, the Three, and the Many: God, Creation, and the Culture of Modernity* (Cambridge University Press, 1993); and Stanley Hauerwas, *A Community of Character: Toward a Constructive Christian Social Ethic* (University of Notre Dame Press, 1981). For a more practical look, see the helpful Hugh Halter and Matt Smay, *The Tangible Community: Creating Incarnational Community* (Jossey-Bass, 2008).

was not all about I. He was about his Father. And he was full of the Spirit, and relied on the Spirit.

The God Who Disagrees

We call this the Trinity. In this way, God is so different from us. For God in his real nature is not individualistic. God is not the iGod. Authentic Jesus community is rehab for idolaters. Because in authentic community, where we are pushed and questioned, we are forced to see ourselves in the mirror with all of our blaring failures. I think you know you have created God in your own image when God approves of everything you do. I once asked a gay friend who goes to the church that I pastor why she keeps coming back week after week. She tells me that she doesn't want to be around spiritual people who agree with her all the time. She also says she definitely doesn't want to hear about a God that always agrees with her lifestyle. Because, she says, that kind of God is probably self-created. After her, my conviction is that the realest form of Christianity is not a club of people who are therapeutically assured that they are perennially right, either by their community or by their God. That, at the end of the day, you know you are probably encountering the real God only to the degree that the God you are encountering disagrees with you. I want to be more like my gay friend. What if every Christian was that tenacious about being confronted with themselves? This is how community forces us to murder our false gods.

Community, in the context of the Trinity, is a return to Eden. The ultimate image of this relational community is Eden. Eden was the first nudist colony. For this reason, in Hebrew, *Eden* means "delight." There, God, Adam, Eve, and all the animals lived nakedly. It is here, somewhere in modern-day Iraq, that God, humans, and creation lived together in pure utopist community. But the community fell apart, undergoing massive changes. At the beginning, there in Eden, we were *naked without shame.* Then after eating some naughty fruit, we were *naked with shame.* Now, after being exiled from Eden, many years later, we're all *clothed with shame*. Our world is Eden backwards. This, sadly, is the story of most of our lives. Because every human wants to go back to Eden. Some have even tried.

A small fringe group of heretics in the early church (frankly, my favorite fringe group) was a group of people called the *Adamites*. Although little tells us about them from history, they are known for believing the only way to worship God in the realest sense was to do so *completely naked*. So they would actually gather together for worship, strip off all their clothes, and try to go worship God commando. Probably rightly so, the early church deemed this a heretical movement. Although most certainly for more practical reasons. Because on a contemporary level, this would undeniably put a chink into the modern worship experience. Try to sing "I Could Sing of Your Love Forever" like *that*. Humans have, since leaving Eden, been trying to reconstitute Eden. And there's a reason. A *very important* reason.

Have you seen the part of *The Lion King* where the dust in the sky actually spells something? When you watch all of the newer animated Disney movies, and have the ability to watch YouTube, you discover there are some really weird things written into some of those movies. There's this scene in *Aladdin* where he sort of comes on to Jasmine. He whispers something to her that is rather inappropriate. It's only possible to see if you know what to look for. In *The Little Mermaid*, the pastor at the wedding on the boat appears to be happy in the southern region. Again, only possible to see if you know what to look for. Then in *The Lion King*, if you watch at the right spot, the dust is stirred up and spells out *SEX* in the sky. Only possible to see if you know what to look for. Again, *if you know what to look for*. Because some guy in a cubical drew that stuff in there. For some reason. And some purpose.

Trinity and Going Commando

The endless human desire for relationship was drawn into the fabric of our lives by a God who is eternally in relationship. For some odd reason, after Eden, we all *stopped going commando*. Eden killed commando. We are all born commando and are buried in a suit. Why? And we might sleep better knowing we don't live in Eden and we've left that place, but that isn't the problem. Because somewhere, at some point in our childhood, at some moment, something happens. All of us yearn to be in real, authentic, powerful communion with God and each other and the rest of the world. Someone once told me that the key to the art of becoming socially comfortable around others is imagining that every time you walk into a room, you are the only one wearing any clothes and everyone else is naked. That was literally the policy in Eden. Community is going commando on a relational level. If you know what to look for, you will discover that our world's desire to find authentic community is something intentional written in the sky. By someone in a cubical. The reality is we may have left Eden, *but Eden has not left us*. And we all yearn, like homesick puppies, to return. To delight. Back to Eden. Luckily, Jesus knows how to get there. He has some directions.

Our first task is to radically embrace a renewed picture of the Trinity—God the Father, Son, and Spirit living in loving embrace. Someone famous once said that *nature is cruel; so, therefore, we can be cruel.* The person who said this based his entire philosophy on the idea that in watching the animal kingdom, with its cruelty and pain and suffering, *we are to be the same.* His name was Adolf Hitler. We all have some picture in our mind of how human relationships should work. This picture is very important. The solution to our idolatry is *not* having *no picture*; it is having a *better picture.* The Trinity is the picture the church has given us for two thousand years. Since God is communal, we too must be communal. It is imperative, in this light, to embrace the notion that the Trinity has never been *an* idea *for* the church in Christian history—it has been *the* idea *of* the church. Therefore, the church is to be the reenactment of the Trinity in a fragmented world. A fourth-century theologian once went so far as to say that if you ever see two human beings *actually* living in *authentic* relationship, you have a glimpse of the Trinity.[5]

Our first task is to learn how to deal with the pain of authentic community. We do this by practicing a holy form of revenge. Jesus was put, history and Scripture tell us, on two blocks of wood with some rusty nails. This image, of God dying, is no doubt a profound one. Now surprisingly, Jesus didn't come out of the tomb with guns blazing, mad at everyone who killed him. *I'm back and I'm pissed.* He very well could have. Especially in the context of a God who sent a flood to start everything over when it wasn't going as planned. In my book, if there ever is a time to pull out the flood card, this is it. After being crucified. He could have. But he didn't. This doesn't mean Jesus didn't have revenge though. This is important. *Jesus did have revenge.* On everyone. It just looked different than our concept of revenge. The human version of revenge looks like retaliation. Someone hurts us and we get back at them Chuck Norris style with a roundhouse kick to the face. Sadly, our kind of revenge is retaliation. But Jesus' revenge is very different. *He called it resurrection.* His way at getting back at the world for killing him was by being raised from the grave. How do we get revenge on people that crucify us? Do we come out with our guns blazing? Or do we come out resurrected? I think one type of revenge works. One doesn't. The important lesson of community is that at some point, if we are faithful to be a part of it, it will deeply scar us.

Scar Wars

In regard to loving people who hurt him, Jesus was a flaming fundamentalist. It's very telling that when Jesus came out of the grave, he came out *showing off his wounds to everyone.* This was a bit of a sticky point for one of the disciples. Thomas, the doubting one, who had a degree in objective scientism, wouldn't believe unless he could put his

---

5. St. Augustine is reported to have said this on a number of occasions.

fingers in the healed holes. He did. And believed. Yet what is profound is this. Now I understand that apparently Jesus, in his divine nature, has the power to do just about anything he wished. Anything. He can start a storm. He can heal a leper. Create a universe. He can end the world. So if Jesus, in his all-powerfulness, can do *anything*, why didn't he come out of the grave without scars? Why leave the scars? What is so important about the healed wounds? In regard to the community Jesus created, *he chose to minister in his woundedness*. Not without it. That is, out of his pain and anguish came his love. Jesus embraces us with his wounded hands. It is a lie to believe that community will make us better people. It won't. Community will hurt us. Truth be told, I have been more hurt by Christians than I have been by any other group in the world. Community won't make us better people; it will make us crucified people. The key is the realization, and the reality, that crucified, *resurrected* people are able to love like Christ did. Some of us simply refuse to resurrect. If we have been crucified, hurt by others in community, and not been resurrected, we are not being Christlike. To be Christlike, in the deepest of senses, is to be crucified *and resurrected*. False community is built on resurrected people who hide their wounds. That is not real resurrection. Real resurrection still shows signs and markings of the pain.

Too darn often, our cultural practice is what I call *Scar Wars*. It is this self-serving thing we do when we all try to one-up each other's hurts and wounds. It's like this endless war to try to be the most hurt possible. You have your scars, sure, *but look at mine*. Relationship can never work, though, in a real sense, when we compare our scars with everyone else's. Some are hurt more than others. Some have been hurt but aren't being honest about it. We must find, somewhere in the person of Christ being made real in our life, a way to focus on the *resurrection* that makes all things right.

What is surprising is how many of us in some form of community are lonely. *Why has God not brought my "Adam" or my "Eve"?* In the economy of Eden, this is not our problem to answer. Adam found his wife by not looking for her. Actually, he found his wife by *going to sleep.* What do you say to a friend who so wants to find a life mate, but just can't? This is one of the most painful things imaginable. I could tell you to make a list, but I don't think that will help. Do what Adam did. Go to sleep. It was while he was asleep that God brought Eve from, well, something inside him, in his dreams. Your Eve, or Adam, isn't meant to be found if you are looking. They are meant to be brought forth, like a miracle. Go to sleep. Trust. Die. If we did a background check on most of our fears, we would find most of them are aberrations.

CPR

Sometimes relationships in community must die. Death is omnipresent in this world. That means it's everywhere. The apostle Paul wrote that he faced it every day.[6] We are literally surrounded by death. We eat dead things. We build houses with dead things. We read Bibles made from dead cows and trees. There are funeral homes and cemeteries everywhere. I have been with two people as they breathed their last breath. You never forget it. Death is losing. It is the realization that something is gone that you can't get back. This one time, a friend of mine came to me after a breakup with his girlfriend of two years. He was devastated. She didn't believe she was supposed to be with him anymore. Losing someone you love is one of the most difficult parts of living, and like anyone else, my friend didn't know what to do. It was as if something was dead. I told him he only had one option. He had to go to the lumber store. And when he got there, he had to ask for two really long pieces of four by four. And he needed to get some nails and a hammer, too. And he needed to take it all home.

When he got home, I told him that he needed to go into the backyard and take the nails and the wood and make a cross. And then

---

6. 1 Corinthians 15:31.

he needed to take the cross and put her on it. And he needed to put nails through her hands and through her feet, *and he needed to crucify her*. Then I said, you know what I mean. Not literally. But spiritually. You need to take this thing, and you need to crucify it. And after this thing is dead, you need to find a cave and put her cold body in it. And then, you need to do the hardest thing in the world. Wait. For three long, dark days. For God to resurrect the dead thing. And the only certifiable way to know if something is to have God's life in it is to put it on the cross and let it die. If it doesn't come back to life, you know God wasn't in it. But if, in three days, or two weeks, or two years, something happens and there is new life, *you know it must be God*. That is called resurrection power. Then I looked him in the face and I told him that the greatest enemy to resurrection is CPR. Resuscitation.

CPR is you and me giving our life to something that is dead. Resurrection is always a possibility. *Always.*

The greatest problem with religion isn't religion; it's what we do to it. Religion is nothing more than the things we do to give our life meaning. I was at a coffee shop this morning reading my Bible and this guy next to me was doing the newspaper crossword. He spent a whole hour doing it. In some form or another, we were both doing devotions. The greatest problem with the Christian religion is that we think it is way more magical than it really is. It isn't magical. It's religion. And religion can't change anything in this world. Christ's resurrection can. Because resurrection gives us hope. And hope doesn't disappoint.

Religion is the Botox of resurrection.

The Botox Gospel

It can give things a lift now, but not for long. In this way, religion is against my religion. Because sometimes we come to religion at the expense of coming to the resurrected Christ. Too many of us are giving CPR to things that God is not resurrecting. Jesus let Judas die. He didn't resurrect him.

Sometimes Jesus lets things die.

Love, in this Jesus way, always goes beyond words. Jesus never says to any of his disciples at any time in the whole of the New Testament, "I love you." Never. Try and find it. It's not there. John, the last gospel written, tells this story where Jesus doesn't *tell* them he loves them but *shows* them he loves them. Jesus washes his disciples' feet. The first person in the Bible to get his feet washed is God. By Abraham at the great trees of Mamre.[7] Years later, I think God loved it so much he wanted to do it for his disciples. This profoundly moving act is the last living act Jesus will perform for his disciples before his death. Now, a couple of comments and observations from the story. First, notice that Jesus is going to wash *all* of his disciples' feet. Including Peter, who will soon deny Jesus, and Judas, who is going to *sell* Jesus to be crucified. The implications of this for us are endless, aren't they? In American Christianity terminology, Judas received Jesus as his Lord and Savior. In totality. Altar call. New believer's packet. Baptism. The whole thing.

As one of Jesus' inner twelve disciples, he had unfettered access to Jesus. In fact, he was the accountant for the disciples. On a number of occasions, he is portrayed as holding the money for the disciples. Jesus had lots of friends who denied him. The first pope did—Peter. I wonder if that is one of the things you put on your résumé if you want to become a pope. Do future popes have to tell the committee about their problems with sin? Second, Jesus *did not* let the disciples wash his feet in return. This is striking. If I were there, it would have been my first goal to get up from having my feet washed and wash Christ's feet, because I don't like receiving without giving back. The picture being offered here is that of the nature of grace. We can only receive. No one is having grace on Jesus. Thirdly, this story, oddly, is in only one of the four gospels. *Not all four.* This is somewhat problematic, because you

---

7. Genesis 18:1–5.

might think all of the gospel writers would have remembered this story and included it.

Here is my theory. John is the last gospel written. Probably like twenty years after the other three. So only the last gospel written includes the story of God washing the feet of those he created. I think it was included in the later gospel because it took them some time to realize how beautifully profound this moment was. *They didn't realize how much they had been loved until years later.* After the fact. Servants never receive praise in their time. It always comes out later. After the obituary.

Many of the writers of the gospels wrote themselves into the stories of Jesus that they themselves wrote. John, in referring to himself in his gospel, always calls himself "the one whom Jesus loved." While the other gospel writers may have taken exception to that, John cleverly writes himself into the story of Jesus. Many people believe the gospel writer Mark also wrote himself into the gospel. When Jesus is captured by the Roman leaders to be executed, Mark's gospel says a man ripped off his clothes and ran from Jesus. The truth is that God cleverly writes himself into the story of those he created. You and me. When God writes himself into our stories, we have to know what to look for. Look for this. Look at your desire to know someone—really *know* someone.

You'll find, too, that Botox is inadequate for that kind of thing.

CHAPTER EIGHT

Milk Cup: Messy Bible

Even Jesus, the author and finisher of our faith, has a hard time finding a publisher. Maybe that's why he never wrote anything.

Google God

Google Earth is creepy. Especially when you search your own house and can see yourself from space. We must look weird to aliens. Especially from *that* angle. My neighbor showed me this thing called Google Earth Street View. There in this tiny blurry picture of the front of his house, my neighbor mows his front yard in freeze-frame. After some research, he found there's this car that Google owns with a camera on top that secretly drives around in front of everyone's houses and takes pictures of them while they mow their lawns. For my neighbor, it just so happened to be that on the random day the Google people drove by his house, he was caught mowing his lawn unawares. So there, on street view, is my neighbor mowing his lawn for the world to see. While part of him enjoyed the attention, having his lawn-mowing practices on stage for public discourse made him a bit uncomfy.

Looking at the picture, I wondered what people thought about my neighbor from that picture. Did they know about his family? Did they think he was a nice guy? Where he shopped for groceries? Because he's a nice guy and all, with a really nice family. But you can only tell so much about my neighbor from that picture on street view. These are things you only get by living next door to the guy. *By knowing him and sharing the same driveway.* Google Earth can only tell you so much about my neighbor. Have you ever seen a picture of someone on the Internet or in a photo album and thought after you meet them how different they look in real life? If you wanted to get acquainted with my neighbor, I'd invite you over to dinner to share a meal, *not* give you a link to Google Earth. Or if I wanted to get to know my wife, I wouldn't do it by sharing a photograph in my wallet. There's a difference between knowing someone and having a picture of them.

There's also a difference between reading about God and knowing God. Reading about God is so important. It can tell you where God is, what other people have encountered in this God, how God mows his lawn, what kind of God he is. But in order to *know* this God, you have to go to where he lives. Or invite him over for dinner. I didn't always know this though.

5:4

Since just before college, I've walked through many stages in my relationship to the Bible. After becoming a Christian, the first person who took time to teach me how to read the Bible was this curmudgeony old Baptist guy with bad breath and lots of time on his hands. While friendly, he was kind of odd and had the social skills of a wood chipper;

but he was kind enough to teach me. *Man, he knew the Bible.* And didn't have much to talk about other than the Bible. Trying to start an actual human-to-human conversation about anything other than the Bible was like developing rapport with a shoe box. It didn't matter to me, though, because he wanted to teach me. We'd meet after church for fifteen minutes in the back by the doughnuts, where he answered my endless questions. If he was stumped, he'd smile and tell me to keep searching. He took the time. People like that change the world more than a thousand books ever could. Some of the stuff he taught me was really weird. He explained how this unknown credit card company (most likely Visa) was led by the antichrist and was going to force everyone to get a chip on their forehead. And when God saw the chip, we'd be toast.

Luckily, at sixteen I had horrible credit, and Visa didn't seem that interested in me. Or my forehead. Another time, my old friend explained to me that God put all the dinosaur bones in the ground to test our faith. To see if we'd really believe the Bible was true. He said that evolution was a lie and if you believed it, you failed the test. While never showing him my cards, I quietly didn't understand. Because he *also* told me Jesus loved me unconditionally and died on the cross for me. I couldn't reconcile the two. A God who loves me and dies for me just didn't seem like the kind of God who'd run around trying to pump-fake everyone into hell. And it made me wonder what *other* things God was trying to pump-fake me into. He may have taught me some weird things, but most importantly, *he taught me the love of the Bible.* That love still lives and breathes.

My newfound love for the Bible quickly matured into a full-blown *obsession.* For a season of time, at four in the morning I'd wake up, light some candles, and read the Bible for a couple of hours before school. The world of the Bible was so enigmatic, so mysterious, so real. Over time, getting up at four paid off. By the time I was twenty-one, I'd memorized the entirety of Mark, Romans, 1 Corinthians, Ephesians,

Colossians, the Timothies, and large portions of Song of Solomon that I had dorky delusions about quoting to my future wife on our wedding night. God was becoming so real to me. This new time of pure obsession was marked by utter devotion to knowing the *real* and *true* meaning of every word in the Bible. And it seemed as though there was one way to understand it. You just had to find it. *If the Bible said it, I believed it.* This also meant that while imperfect people like David and Peter had written it, it was imagined that God spoke into one ear while their pen transcribed what he said. Someone taught me along the way some new vocabulary, to help me explain to others what I'd come to think about this perfect Bible. Some of these words were *infallible* and *inerrant.* This was a very fruitful stage of life for me. And I learned lots of great things about God.

The day things began to change is unforgettable. Having just entered seminary after finishing Bible college, a new world of creative ideas knocked at the door regarding the Bible, faith, theology, and Christian history. One day, reading the book of John for my morning reading time, I came across a startling discovery. My translation of the Bible didn't have a verse: John 5:4. It just skipped from John 5:3 to John 5:5. Soon I discovered that other people's Bible, much to my surprise, didn't have the verse either. *It was simply missing.* There was this local Bible radio program I listened to with this guy I really respected. Having never called in before, I rang him one afternoon while his show was on air and asked him why the Bible I'd paid for didn't come with John 5:4. After I listened to him flip through his Bible on the air, he told me he would send me a personalized off-air tape to respond. He explained how sorry he was that he couldn't answer this very important question on the air. Two weeks later, I got a cassette tape in the mail. In it, he told me it was admirable that I'd ask such a compelling question. *Then he told me that I should simply ignore the problem and move on.* Because the problem shouldn't affect my faith.

At first it didn't. But the question just sat in me like a sock under the bed collecting dust. And I noticed some things changing inside of me. Lots of factors played in. The books I was reading at the time talked about how the Bible had gone through somewhat of a process to get where it is today. It wasn't simply written and dropped from heaven. As well, Christian friends were confidentially sharing with me their personal problems with the Bible; how it was starting to be more challenging to come to grips with than before. For the first time ever, I was finding sitting through sermons more difficult as I'd fester with cynicism, feeling that the preacher wasn't being more honest about questions regarding the Bible. It started to feel as though I'd been fed a lie. This turned to bitterness.

Soon I got really depressed, contemplated throwing the Bible aside, and almost quit Christianity entirely. Yet I still loved Jesus. With everything. So I had to make a choice.

Be it as it may, after a season of intense personal questioning, I decided that the Bible was not Jesus. In no way was I questioning Jesus; *I just knew the Bible was not Jesus.* It was sad. Like someone had died. It felt like I had stabbed the Bible in the back. Or that I'd thrown it out. It felt like I was the one who broke up with it, and I watched as it cried itself to sleep. *You don't believe in me anymore.* Like I really didn't believe anymore. That I was a heretic for having questions. I didn't tell friends out of fear they would agree with my own suspicions about myself. Then I met someone who reintroduced me to the Bible. His name was Martin Luther.

Why Protest?

In a seminary class on Christian history, we started discussing the process that it took for the Bible to get where it is today; from writing, to selection, to publishing. The professor's name was Dan. We discussed how the church has, for thousands of years, been living in relationship and covenant with this book. We learned that humans have wrestled with the Bible's place in faith for some time now. That is, my problems

were nothing new. Nearly half a century ago, risky questions began
erupting over the Bible's authority and its purpose in faith. These
questions led to some of the most painful and profound divisions in
the Christian church ever. *It was profoundly sad to me that the Bible
was dividing Christians, not uniting them.* Dan started talking about
some important things that happened in the sixteenth century. Back
then, some four hundred years ago, the Scriptures were in short supply
and were read largely only by the clergy, bishops, and priests. This was
because, first, many people couldn't read, and, second, Roman Catholic
tradition reserved the right to interpret the Bible. Also, church services
might as well have been in Chinese. At that time, Mass was conducted
only in Latin. Now, there's no problem with Latin except that basically
no normal human being knew it. It's like going to church in America
and being expected to sit through a one-hour sermon in Swahili. You
think you're not getting fed at church? Also, people paid overwhelming
sums of money to the church for forgiveness and absolution of sins.
They called these *indulgences*. Positively, they paid for some of the
most incredible church buildings ever constructed. But negatively,
it appeared to be pushing people from God and the church. Johann
Tetzel, a sixteenth-century proponent of indulgences, coined a phrase:
"As soon as the coin in the coffer rings, a soul from purgatory springs."
Even more so, this was at a time when a really long line of popes had
quite a bad rap sheet. Suffice it to say, like it always has been, the church
was sick. And in this context, a man started asking some big and
painful questions inside the church.

Martin Luther was a Roman Catholic monk who also became a
theology professor and pastor; he had a heart for truth and people.[1] Those
who have written about him believe that he was severely depressed and
probably had major sexual issues to boot. Those closest to him describe

---

1. The best biography to date is the monolithic *Here I Stand: A Life of
   Martin Luther* by Roland H. Bainton (Abingdon-Cokesbury, 1950).

how he constantly worried that the devil was after him and God was always mad at him. He even doubted that God could redeem someone as sick and screwed up as he was. The story goes that one night he was walking down the road in a rainstorm and lightning struck, almost killing him. Later, after this run-in with death along with other experiences, Luther was reading the book of Romans and realized that God wasn't as mad at him as he thought. This new idea was birthed in him. Grace. Grace *alone.* And he believed the way to tap into this was by faith. This changed everything for him. Because in the context of this idea of grace, God loved him undeniably because of Jesus' death and resurrection.

After this, Luther started to get antsy about some practices of his church such as indulgences, the popes, and why normal people couldn't read the Bible on their own. One evening, after stirring and stewing on this for some time, Luther wrote a set of ninety-five questions and ideas (known as theses) for debate and nailed them up on the door of a church in a town called Wittenberg in Germany. This was a common practice back then, with nothing particularly unusual about it. The date was All Hollow's Eve, October 31, 1517. Yet this time for some reason, copies of the document were printed and widely distributed. Luther apparently had an easier time finding a publisher than Jesus did. Word spread across the German countryside of a question-raiser. People discussed and debated the questions that he had posted. Then someone told the pope in Rome. It didn't take long for Pope Leo the Tenth to get an ulcer. And now that Luther was on his radar, confrontation was inevitable. One of these confrontations, called the Diet of Worms, gave Luther a venue to believe that the pope should no longer have the right to be the only interpreter of Scripture. And that everyone should be able to read it. Why? Because he was "held captive" by this thing called the Bible. For the pope, the Bible and its interpretation was something the church did. For Luther, *everyone* should be able to read the Scriptures for themselves and understand them. Eventually, and probably for good reason, Luther was excommunicated from the church for his insubordination. After the Diet of Worms, Luther changed his name to Junker George and went into hiding; sitting in a room for months, he translated the Bible into German for the people in the pew whom he loved. The people who followed Luther got a name. Later, someone called these people *protestantes*, meaning "protesters," which with time was capitalized and became Protestants.

There were negatives to this whole movement that Luther began. People showed themselves rather violent when they became freed from the authority of the pope. Hans Küng, a contemporary Roman Catholic, famously said that at the end of the day, when Luther dethroned the pope, he and the people who followed him unintentionally enthroned a Paper Pope: *the Bible*. Now that the normal, everyday person could read and interpret the Bible, a series of wars began erupting over this book. No doubt the world today is better because the Bible is in the public domain (at least some versions of it are). But we have also failed to get along with each other. *Ironically, the more that people have the Bible in their hands, the less they agree with each other.*

Today, everyone seems to believe theirs, and *only* theirs, is the right interpretation of the Bible. Depending on *their* translation. Of which we have a million. Have you noticed we have a Bible for everyone? We have a Bible for moms. One for moms of twins. One for moms with twin athletes. A Bible for moms with twins who have athlete's foot.[2] I think we are in a new season today. Most people are looking to themselves as their own pope. We have moved from the Pope, to the Paper Pope, to the iPope. We have a Burger King way of reading Scripture; we always have it our way. We have become our own popes.

All of this stuff about Luther seemed to complicate things for me. Dan said that Luther had a *very* high view of the Scriptures and argued that everyone should have the ability to read them on their own. Yet at

---

2. My friend Curt Harlow tells this joke much better than I do. But he said I could use it.

the same time, Luther openly struggled with elements of the Bible that didn't make clear sense to him. For instance, Luther couldn't stand the book of James and wanted it taken out of the Bible, calling it an *epistle of straw*. Luther also thought the book of Esther was too Jewish and that it "Judaized."[3] It still surprises many that he even questioned if some of the books we had in the Bible were written by the people we think they were written by. He was almost sure Peter didn't write 2 Peter. But for Luther, this didn't matter. The issue wasn't whether it was written by this or that person. The issue was *if it preached Christ and him crucified*. This is why Luther even removed a number of books from the Protestant Bible, what the Protestants call the Apocrypha. Regardless of who wrote them, he did not believe these books preached the grace of Christ.

Now for Luther, at the end of the day, *he still held the Bible as God-breathed* and *inspired*. Because for him, *just because it was inspired didn't mean you swept your questions under the rug*.[4] Dan told us that Luther wrestled with the Scriptures—still lived under them—but clung to Jesus with all of his heart. As I read Luther, I found that he, like me, had some questions about the Bible, still loved Jesus wholeheartedly, and wanted others to know that Jesus. And he was *entirely* enthralled with the grace of Christ on a sinner like himself. Then one day, it dawned on me. Luther's understanding of the Bible began to help me in the midst of my problems of understanding the Bible.

What I found in Luther is what I needed: *a low view of himself, a high view of Scripture, and an even higher view of Jesus.*

---

3. Sadly, at the end of his life, Luther became somewhat of a nutso. He became rather anti-Semitic. In 1543, one of his last writings, Luther wrote *Von den Jüden und ihren Lügen* (modern spelling) or *On the Jews and Their Lies.*

4. A model of doing this is found in the ever-helpful and brilliant Donald G. Bloesch, *Holy Scripture: Revelation, Inspiration and Interpretation*, Christian Foundations 2 (Downers Grove, IL: InterVarsity Press, 1994). Bloesch is incredible. Eat him up.

Following Luther's practice meant I was free to have a brain—to think, to wonder, and to dream. *I didn't have to have a rug to sweep questions under.* Following Luther meant Jesus was above the Bible, and that the Bible was not the ruler of the heavens. And following Luther meant the Bible was the model for how to find Jesus. It would be a lie if we said everything about or in the Bible made sense to us. But that's quite all right. Because we don't worship it. Now questions about the Bible are always in the context of a larger love for God. It is in the freedom of being honest about this that new levels of relationship are possible.

Eating the Menu

Somebody told me she thinks the whole Jesus thing is a great idea. It's the Bible that she didn't get. It didn't make sense to her why the Bible has to be in the whole equation. Why couldn't we just stick to Jesus and forget the Bible? I told her this probably wasn't possible. It's like jumping on turtles. There's this secret level in Super Mario, the first one, with Duck Hunt, where you can jump on this turtle over and over and you can get a million lives. My best friend in fourth grade, Blair, told me about this. Quickly, as soon as I could, I went home after school to find it. I couldn't find the place. Jumping on all the wrong turtles over and over. It was deflating. These eternal-life turtles were nowhere to be found. So I called Blair and had him come over and show me. Blair came over and showed me right where it was. I couldn't find the extra lives without him. I explained to my friend that to understand how the Bible fits in with Jesus, you need to replace Blair with the Bible. Jesus is real and powerful and gives real *eternal life*—here and now and in the future. Our problem isn't that there isn't real life—*it's that we can't find it on our own.* We need someone to show us the way. The Bible is Blair. It shows us the way. Because God is beyond you. The Bible is the thing that points you to the guy who knows God because he is God. The Bible isn't God though. And you can't find eternal life on your own.

Someone else told me that the Bible is like a menu. It's a listing of all the stuff in the kitchen. It makes getting your food easier. Imagine the difficulty of getting the food you wanted if the waitress had to explain everything by mouth. But we can't eat the menu. Because it's not about the menu. The Bible is like a menu. It is the thing that gets the stuff in the kitchen to you. Some people think it's all about the menu. I don't think so. The menu is the middleman. It gets the stuff we need to us. Some of us are eating the menu. But that's not what gives life.

My Relic

In retrospect, looking back to my childhood, I'm pretty sure I never saw the real Santa Claus. *Pretty sure.* How could one know? In a sea of fake Santas, how could one be sure it was the *real* one? Very early on, I became an apologist for the real Santa. When someone at recess claimed to have seen him, *the real him*, there was a litmus test to determine the legitimacy. Did you pull on his beard? Were there elves? Was he fat? Because for being the battle-tested purist that I was, there was only one connection to the real Santa. Christmas morning. Nothing else. And if we were all honest with ourselves, we'd admit this was the only real encounter any of us really had with the real Santa. Everything else was a hoax. We all knew those imposters at the mall were in it for the money. Christmas morning became everything. *Everything.*

I had it down to a science. Here was the protocol. In bed at 8:00 PM sharp in case he came early and got done in Canada faster than I'd calculated. Never ever drink water that night, to keep from going to the bathroom in the middle of the night, so as to not scare him off in case he's already there. And never, under any circumstance, ever build a fire on Christmas Eve. My parents built Christmas up too, to make the whole thing more magical. I'll never forget the moment my parents told me there was no Santa Claus. It made no sense, like someone trying to explain that the cereal I ate that morning never really existed. It was utter heresy. There were two stages when they told me. The first was thinking something along the lines of, "These people are deceived and have lapsed into unbelief. How could they fall away? Even my parents have fallen away." But then reason arose, and what can I say: I cried hard and for a long time. I wondered why my parents let me believe in something so false. Part of it I think was that they didn't want to crush me. But more importantly, I don't think I could have handled it. My whole world would have crumbled. Let's face it: had they told me any earlier, I wouldn't have believed them, no matter what they said. *Santa was real.* I knew. Because there was always Christmas morning—the gifts. What about the presents? Where did those come from? What about all the presents I had gotten?

I still remember the magic before they let me down. Stumbling down the stairs, slipping like a drunken sleepwalker in my socks on the hardwood floor, I'd pass the kitchen table where a plate of warm cookies and cold whole milk had been placed the night before. It was our little family ritual. And always, before we got in the living room, we would pass the cookies and milk. If we'd played our cards right, the empty plate and glass would be a sign of things to come. It was like a glass ball predicting my future loot. I'd pass by and glance, heart fluttering, to see if the cookies had in fact been eaten. *Would Santa partake of my chocolate chip offering?* Of course, now the warm cookies had become cold, hard, and half-eaten. And the milk, lukewarm and half chugged, had a mouth ring of dried milk residue around the rim. *This was the best part.* It was like we stood on holy ground. Of course they were never fully eaten. Just half of them. The point was his presence, not Santa's eating problem. For heaven's sake, Santa might be hungry, but he's still a gentleman, and no doubt had a waist to watch. Every Christmas, the lip marks of dried milk residue on the rim stirred me into transcendental wonder. Nothing else all year got me like that. I remember thinking, *Santa's lips were on this.* Not only that, but the milk from *our* container could still be on his lips right now over China or something. This inspired me to no end. Then, in the moment of magic, I would reach out, trembling fingers and all, to feel a lukewarm glass touched by Santa himself just hours, maybe minutes, earlier. And boy, if magic exists, this is what it's like. It was like a child reaching into history, into hope, into real existence. "He was just here," I would say. And my parents would look in my eyes and nod, leading me into the den of loot. Yet after all the fanfare of gifts and breakfast, entranced by the milk-stained glass and cookies, I'd go back to the cup Santa touched.

It was so incredible knowing something before me, this very cup and cookie, had actually *touched* the very One. Santa was here. So with precision and care, I'd sneak the cup up to my room and enshrine it on my bed stand. They were relics, a sort of window to the divine if you will. They were autographs of truth. And every night, with a humble and contrite heart, I'd stare at it, next to my bed. Because, well, Santa touched these very things before me. Everyone else had "seen" Santa, or at least a fake one. At least here it was authentic. There was a connection. If I looked closely, I could see his fingerprints on the glass. It was powerful. It became my Santa Claus. And in the absence of Santa, I had the cup with his lip stains. Cup and cookie became Santa. The cup was safer than Santa. It was a relic. Something that pointed to the real thing.

The Bible is safer than God. And there is a reason we put it in the place of God. There's a reason we do it. *Because we can't thumb through, highlight, put little cloth string in the middle of, put a weird map at the end, cover in leather, or actually touch God.* God will never work as a doorstop or fall in between the cracks of our cars. You can put verse numbers to the Bible, not God. God has no 1:1. There is no 2nd God. And so, because we can touch it, feel it, and flip through it, we accept our Bible as our personal Lord and Savior and turn it into our God. But there is only one problem with that. It violates the first commandment God gave through Moses. No god (small *g*) before God (big *G*). Like the cup with the stains, the Bible points to *someone who has been here*. And yet the Bible isn't God. There is a God who existed long before the Bible did.

Jesus is my favorite pope.

CHAPTER NINE

Ending My Atheism: Messy Suffering

This God needs Kleenex.

A man gets into a fender bender as he pulls out for work in the morning. Everyone else was fine, but the man bumped his head on the steering wheel because he never wore his seat belt. The man's wife was ticked. The car, a new green minivan, cost them everything. After a trip to the hospital to check the small bump on his head, they discover from the head scan that the man has a brain tumor. The accident, as much as it sucked, was what saved him. It gave him years of real life afterward—after they removed the tumor. His wife was happy then. We are all the wife in the story. We get mad at the pain of life. We hate the inconvenience. It makes life painful. But suffering ultimately forces us to see ourselves for real. Inside. And it often brings healing.

Why

Like the weather, our lives are so ridiculously unpredictable. Aren't they? Everything, at times, seems up in the air. In question. But maybe that's how we learn to fly. It's when we're grounded that things are too safe, too predictable, like getting your kicks from waiting and watching for the mailman. Sometimes predictability leads to a slow and enveloping death. Death by safety. Someone once said that boats are safe in a harbor; *the problem is, that's not what boats are made for.* Humans aren't made for the harbor either. Nor is God. Harbored people rarely, if ever, change the world. Do they? But then again, our world increasingly thinks that those who fly are out there and have their heads in the clouds. It seems as though the mantra of the contemporary world is to be middle of the road; be safe, be prepared. Be balanced. We are an insured people. But there's this secret energy in each of us that seeks to rebel. An energy that pulls us to something *out there*. Into the dark. Into the unseen. Maybe that is the essential nature of humanity.

What other living creature, when asked why it searches the dark world, why it wanders the earth to see a glacier, why it wants to explore space, answers, "Because." Just to do it. We are the creatures of "because." For no apparent reason. Just "because." Maybe that "because" is actually there for something bigger. More incredible. Something mysterious. We are also the only ones that ask of the nature of things, why? Why does the world exist? Why am I lonely? Why is life so hard? Have you ever wondered about these things?

Humans seem to be thirsty for something different. Looking for something out there. Something behind it all. Why has the news on the television been so hard to watch this year? I already don't think it's smart to watch the news on TV, because they only have half-hour segments to cover *all* of the stories around the globe in a nice compartmentalized newscast. It seems wrong, in our guts, that we follow a story about genocide with Bob at the sports desk. This is why I read the newspaper instead. Although it's fun to watch those tanned news people, makeup and suits and all, perfectly reading us the news off some teleprompter. They make it look a little *too* sexy. At least with the newspaper, you can start a fire with it afterward. Recently, in the newspaper, a number of young people have been biographied. Many of them ended their own life. Others are in counseling. But they all have one thing in common. They were all *bullied*. One college kid from the East Coast abruptly ended his own life because someone secretly taped him and another man in his dorm room in a moment of intimacy and plastered it all around the Internet without his permission. Under the pressure of not having told his friends and family that he was gay, the college boy killed himself. It was all over the news for weeks.

After this, a swath of other stories came out. Kids right and left seemed to feel they could now tell their story about being *bullied* in school for their skin color, their sexuality, their religion, or other things. We all remember moments like this when we were kids, when we could say we were bullied. They were deeply shameful and powerful moments in our life. It may comfort the families of kids who ended their own lives, to know that Jesus was equally bullied. It may comfort kids of yours in school who are bullied that Jesus gets it. If crucifixion isn't the ugliest form of bullying, what is? During the time of Jesus, popular religion always depicted God on the side of the winners. God was the victor for the Greeks. God was the powerful force of the rich. God stood on the side of the powerful. People didn't appreciate what Jesus was trying to do for a number of reasons. But what was utter foolishness to the Greeks was that Jesus claimed to be God *and then went and died*. It was ridiculous to think that God could lose. Let alone be the God of the losers. As the God of the losers, Jesus was on the side of the oppressed. Jesus embraced the marginalized. Jesus wept for the dead. Jesus hugged the dirty. It was his method of love. And it worked.

Jesus gathered the *bullied* and started a church with them.

It was Jesus who over and over again stood on the side of the oppressed. He stood with the people, *not Rome*. The peasant, *not religious powers*. The harlot, *not the law*. Let me put it on the school playground. When we pick teams for a kickball tournament at recess, we pick the two people who get to choose those on their teams. The team captains. And then we always pick the biggest, the smartest, the wisest, the most powerful first, don't we? Yes, if we want to win. If we want to lose, what do we do? We ask those in the front wanting to be picked first, and look for the *scrawniest, weakest, dumbest* person we can find. Then we pick him and the rest of his friends. That's doing it Jesus-style. Jesus picked the weakest and stood up for them. No matter their sexuality. No matter their occupation. No matter their religious tradition. He still does that.

Koan

My dad is a Buddhist. When we're together, we talk about truth and religion and politics. I've learned a lot from my dad. And hopefully he's learned something from his Christian son. There is this Buddhist tradition called *koan*. In koan, a Buddhist learner is asked a profound question about life by a teacher. Kind of a Yoda and Luke sort of thing. The learner, after being asked a question, thinks about the question intensely. But they are not allowed to answer the question. All they can do is just think about the question. And the question, *not the answer*, is believed to arouse a sense of spiritual awareness within the learner. In koan, the truth is in the question. I'm not a Buddhist, but I think suffering is like that.

Suffering is Christ's koan to the world.

It makes us ask why. We always think suffering has to have an answer. That we can explain *why* it happened. Non-Christian friends of mine ask all the time, "How can you believe in a God that lets suffering happen?" And I get that question. It's overasked, but I get it. Sometimes I wonder if there is, like, this secret class that every nonreligious person takes where they learn that question. And the professor tells everyone, "Hey, if you ask Christians this question, they'll realize there is no answer and implode." Truth is, *I have no idea why God lets suffering happen*. But I know one thing. Every person I know who suffers asks that question. Where is God in this? What if the beauty is in the question? Not the answer. What if there is no answer to that question? Sure, we could fashion some really incredible answer to that question. We could have our own class on how to answer this question. Someone says, "How can you believe in a God that lets suffering happen?" Then the Christian professor says, "Tell the pagan this. How can you not believe in a God that invented Vermont maple syrup? Then they will believe!" The class will go out, empowered with truth to tell others to make all suffering people believe. But for someone who is truly suffering, they are not actually looking for an answer. They are simply wanting to ask the question. The message of Jesus is not that he brings answers to the suffering. No. Jesus brings presence to the suffering. He is with them. And it is for that reason, in our suffering, that we begin to ask deeply profound questions about the nature of the universe. God is right there, suffering alongside us.

The People Who Show Up to Funerals

What if in the story of humanity the question *why* is proof of some higher power? In the story of Job, perhaps the oldest story in the Bible, we encounter the most profound understanding of suffering in the Bible.[1] Job, the most righteous man in the East, loses everything. Well, *almost* everything. His family. His farm. His goats. His dignity. His respect. He loses so much. But not everything. After a couple of days of sitting in the dust, trying to figure God out in the whole thing, his three friends come to him. This is how suffering usually goes. We lose everything that we actually like; then our three friends come to us with trite advice about *why* this all happened. We call this a funeral.

---

1. For a great commentary on the book of Job, see David J. A. Clines, *Job 1–20*, Word Biblical Commentary (Word, 1989).

Now here is what scares me. All of their answers are deeply religious answers. "You weren't faithful to God." "God must be mad at you." "God is trying to teach you something." When my wife's dad died, it was incredible.

All of Job's friends came to his funeral.

They told her everything was going to be all right. God planned this all out. God is in it. God wanted this to happen. She would listen and bite her lip. It struck me that most of the religious things people said to her made God look really mean. The lesson of Job is how insufficient religious answers are for suffering. Theology can never explain *why* God allows suffering. In the story of Job, bad theology is often the thing that makes suffering unbearable. And how human-to-human presence is what people need. Someone to sit in the dirt with. The beautiful part of the story is Job's response to suffering. He responds by hitting the dirt. And in the dirt, after shaving his hair off and ripping off his clothes, he *worships*. That is striking when you consider that humans, in the story of creation, are nothing more than dirt that breathes. Job is incredible. Suffering leads to dirt. Dirt leads to worship. So suffering takes us back to who we really are. Dirt.

The Plagiarism of Worship

This connection between worship and suffering continues in the story of Scripture. In the story of Jonah, the prophet gets swallowed by a fish. Once he is safe and sound in the digestive tract of a large fish, Jonah sings a song. In beautiful Hebrew poetry, Jonah cries out to God in his suffering. Now, what is striking isn't the way the song sounds but the words he chooses to use. If you were to look at the words he sang in the belly of the fish and then go and read a spattering of the psalms, you would give a double take. Almost cut and paste, Jonah sings the songs of the psalms in the belly of the fish. In the music world, we call this plagiarism. In the Bible, we call it worship. The Bible is a book of worship for sufferers. It is God giving us words to sing in light of

our suffering. What if our worship was more like Jonah in the belly
of a fish than a typical worship service at church? I think our songs
would be more about our suffering than our successes. I already feel
too uncomfortable with so much of the music we sing in church. Too
much of our worship toward God is about us. Look at how many of our
worship songs start with the word *I*. This one time, I was singing this
song at church and started actually listening to what I was saying. It was
about how I would never leave Jesus. How I'd never forsake him. How
I would be this perfect little follower. Then I stopped singing. Because
none of those things are true. I will forsake Jesus. I won't be perfect. I
may leave Jesus. Who knows? Listen, if Judas could, you could too.

Like a thesaurus, there are many words for *worship* in the Bible.[2] The
Hebrews in the Old Testament speak of worship as *shachah*. To bow
down; to lower oneself; to get in the dust. The Greeks used a different
word that the writers used in the New Testament: *proskyneō*. *Proskyneō*
is the same thing Judas did to Jesus when he led the Roman soldiers to
where he was. With a guard of Roman soldiers, Judas runs up to Jesus
and *proskyneōs* him. *He kisses him*. Worship, *proskyneō*, is to kiss toward
someone. It's a big sloppy kiss. I've done lots of weddings in my life,
and I've noticed something. Standing there in front of the two people
preparing to live life together, you quickly discover that every kiss is
different. Some kisses are what I call home-school kisses. Like they had
never kissed before. Others are cootie kisses, like the guy is afraid of
catching something. But they are all different. Worship is not always
the same for people. Why do we feel like we *have* to raise our hands in

---

2. Three great books on *worship* that I would recommend are *Worship by the
Book*, edited by D. A. Carson, with Mark Ashton, R. Kent Hughes, and
Timothy J. Keller (Zondervan, 2002); and by Marva J. Dawn, *Reaching
Out Without Dumbing Down: A Theology of Worship for the Turn-of-
the-Century Culture* (Eerdmans, 1995) and *A Royal Waste of Time: The
Splendor of Worshiping God and Being Church for the World* (Eerdmans,
1999).

worship? We raise our hands in worship, but Job dropped himself to the dirt when he worshipped. Worship, in this sense, shouldn't be judged on how excited we get. Some raise hands. Some drop to the floor. Some bark like dogs. Potato, potahto. My paraplegic friend can't move her arms. Is she not worshipping God?

Pain, suffering, toil; these things cause us to ask big questions of God. A little kid at a summer camp asked me if it was okay to be mad at God. To ask God big questions that may hurt God. I told the girl about this time when Jesus was crucified and how at the end of his life he screamed out one of the psalms. With the words of Psalm 22 on his lips, *"Eloi, Eloi, lama sabachthani?"* there was clarity on the topic. Jesus asked God at his death, "God, why have you left me?"[3] For a number of reasons, this song choice intrigues me. To begin, Jesus is seemingly willing to utter things that make both the writers of the Bible and our own theological heads swim, especially as it deals with his relationship to the Father. I love his honesty. It's spiritually cathartic. The earliest Christians wrestled mostly with how Jesus was or was not God, and his relationship to his "Father" was deeply important, too. This was because Jesus said very important yet confusing things about this, like "I and the Father are one."[4] The gospel writers made equally confusing statements about Jesus' relationship to his Father: "In the beginning was the Word [Jesus], and the Word was with God [the Father], and the Word was God. He was with God in the beginning."[5] But just when it looked like the theological shirt was ironed, he ruffles it up at the end with his last song on the cross. And frankly, this last record of his conversation with the voice from heaven makes it a little less cut and dried. How could Jesus be abandoned by this voice in heaven? Is that possible?

But moreover, Jesus, in his death, teaches a class for the world on a

---

3. Matthew 27:46.
4. John 10:30.
5. John 1:1–2.

subject very few Christians have chosen to enroll in. In his final breath, with no more air in his lungs and few friends on the ground, Jesus utters a really hard question to this voice in the sky. He basically says, "Why have you ditched me?" And this is directed to God. Whew. I mean this is a *really* hard question. A question that makes the angels, and those at the cross, stop and do a double take. As is the case with this one, not only are these kinds of questions hard, but they are the kind of questions that don't get answered. I told the girl at summer camp that followers of Jesus must live knowing both that their questions should be hard and yet most likely won't get answered, *especially if some of the questions in red in the Bible are the same as theirs.*

Jesus modeled honesty in his prayers.

Back to why I don't like the TV. It's weird how quickly I change the channel when the pictures of the kids from Africa with the flies on their mouths come on. We all change the channel. Have you ever thought about how that makes you feel? The feeling in your gut? The Trinity, incarnation, and the nature of the hypostatic union don't always make sense to me, but it never ceases to surprise me that seeing children with flies on their lips makes me feel pain. Evolution can't explain that. Suffering is God's subliminal message to the world that he still hides behind the scenes. The fact that people ask how we can believe in a God in the midst of suffering is proof that suffering causes us to ask big questions about God. Jesus wept when one of his best friends died. This is the Kleenex-God.

The Fastest-Growing Denomination

The fastest-growing Christian denomination in the United States is called cynicism.

It pervades every element of Christian spirituality. I actually think cynicism is proof that God exists. We get so cynical about church because God lives in us and tells us stuff about the church, things that are wrong about it, and we know he's right. We see that the pastor drives a $200,000 car and people don't have food. We see things that make our hearts cringe with anger. That is why I think cynicism toward church proves there is a God. Remember how the story of God's Spirit hovering over creation eventually comes to a brilliant culmination after Jesus goes to heaven? In Acts 2, that same Spirit stops *hovering* and *descends* to live in all the believers. And when it happens, someone at the prayer meeting stands up and reads a story from the Old Testament that promised this would happen. And the story says that the Spirit would come on everyone, and they would all—men and women, children and adults—*be prophets*. Like Moses. Like Nathan. Like Samuel. Like Jesus.

The Spirit of prophesy that lived in all the Old Testament prophets would live in all of us today, telling us about justice and righteousness and what is good and evil in the world. That is why our problem isn't church. The problem is that we don't know how to fix it. That is the problem. You can't. I can't. Max Lucado can't. Donald Miller can't. Bono can't. No one can fix the church. It's unfixable in the same way you can't fix the foundation of your house without ripping it apart. So when we see stuff, we recognize it. Then, after a long time of inaction, it turns into something very dangerous, very evil, very destructive. We call it cynicism. But before it was cynicism, it was revelation. It was prophesy. It was seeing something God was saying. Cynicism is fermented revelation gone bad. We get cynical because other people aren't doing the things to help that we ourselves know we are supposed to do. The problem is, cynics don't change the world. They just make it more miserable. Or let me put it this way. You think *you* have reason to be cynical. Talk about *God* having a reason to be cynical. Jesus kept going to church. That's because had he not, no one would have listened to him. You are mad because churches don't listen to what you have to say, and you never commit to living life with them. How hypocritical. That's like telling your teacher to change her teaching style, because you are different, by never going to class. In God's kingdom, commitment and willingness to act are required to speak. There are no armchair prophets in this kingdom.

Why do we become cynical? The cynical are stuck in an aquarium. Feeling pain is central to Christian spirituality. On the Oregon coast, we have many different kinds of weird animals. Seagulls. Jellyfish. Those little crabs in the sand. And sea anemones. The ones in the wild are crazy. When I was little, I went on a field trip and the guide told us that if we put our finger in the mouth of the sea anemone, very softly, they will think it is food and hold on with their sticky little fingers. He was right. If you softly put your finger into a wild sea anemone it will try to eat your finger. After we stuck our fingers in the wild sea anemones, we went to the Oregon Coast Aquarium. There they had a petting zoo of domesticated sea anemones. We were allowed to touch them too. These anemones were way different. Because they had been poked so many times, they didn't bite on your finger. It is like they look up at you and say, "Do you think I'm a moron? That's not food. Why not try taking your finger out of my throat?" At the aquarium, the anemones have lost their ability to respond because they have been poked so many times. So many humans are in the aquarium. They have lost heart because they have been hurt so many times. Jesus tries to heal people like that so they can care again. Jesus people can get hurt because he took them from the aquarium and put them in the wild again. They are free. And they can feel pain. Had pain been a sin, Jesus most likely would not have cried out from the cross in shattering pain. Pain is human. Humanity is pain. To ignore pain is to be a nonhuman. It is to be an alien. Christians embrace pain because they have been crucified with Christ.

There are plenty of arguments against the existence of God. But for me, suffering is not one of them. Pain, tears, and loss all force us to ask the deepest questions about our world. It's understandable why so many people are mad at God. God let their child die. God let his girlfriend cheat on him. God let people die without food. I get it. I heard someone say that you can't be mad at God and still not believe in him. It sounds a little weird, but I think it's true. There are other, better arguments against God's existence. Maybe the greatest argument against God is his people. The church.

The New Blessing

My friend Dan, who spends his life studying the history of Christianity, tells me that if we knew what it meant, none of us would want to be blessed. We throw the word around, he says. Bless you. Bless America. God bless. Once he looked at the writings of the earliest Christians and found that they too used the word. But it wasn't in the same way we do. When we in the twenty-first century think about being blessed, we think of cars. Of money. Of white picket fences. Blessing for Americans equals stuff. Dan told me that the earliest Christians would bless each other and called themselves blessed. But it was for the opposite reason we do. For them, to be blessed meant you suffered with Jesus. That you were persecuted for his name. That your family was torn apart because of the gospel. That you were hurt for your faith. And if you experienced all of these, *you were blessed*. To share in the suffering of Jesus was to be a blessed people. In our world, to share in the empire's abundance is to be blessed.

I think Jesus is a crutch. People rely on it. They lean on it. They assume it. It's an easy way out of having to see things in our world that point to God. We all have a crutch. I also think atheism is a crutch. So is being a Republican. So is joining a yoga group or Elks lodge. We all lean on something. It just happens to be that the best crutch I have found is Jesus. All the other crutches failed me.

Christians are repentant atheists.

CHAPTER TEN

Foreplay: Messy Theology

At the end of the day, everyone goes about it differently.

Theology and the Art of Egg Ordering

Some take them over easy. Others over hard. Some poached. It's a free-for-all really. But where did we learn how to order eggs? Nowhere on the accessible menu is a helpful explanation of how to order an egg or what to expect. We're just supposed to know what we want. No class covers it. We're simply left to our own primal human devices. Yet somewhere along the way in the human experience, it's assumed we just pick up this important skill. Like a caveman discovering fire. I'm always a little caught off guard when the waitress questions me about my egg preference in the morning. There are so many options to choose from. Over hard. Boiled. Scrambled. Benedict. I kind of feel put on the spot, underscored by the general lack of training. So feeling rushed, I just respond. Sometimes it seems like I'm just throwing adjectives in there. Over easy; *complacent and melancholy*. We need a book to know our options as the egg-eating public. I'd buy it. *Over Not-So-Easy: Contemporary Egg Ordering Options in a Postmodern Milieu*. I was thinking about it. There's two central ways we learn how we like our eggs done. First, and most common, we learn from someone who's been there before. This is usually a mother or father figure. Earlier in life, on our behalf, they would order for us, speeding up the whole process and giving us the freedom to worry about the eating part. It's a symbiotic relationship. Because we don't care and just want the eggs, we abrogate such authority to those who know what is best.

Then we got older. This is where the rubber meets the egg-road. In our early adult years, we ultimately learn what we like a second way—by making a long list of egg mistakes. It's only after trying over easy that you discern an acute sense that runny yellow slime isn't your cup of tea before ten. And luckily, after you've made the mistake, you never will again. But it's still tricky. If only the waitress wasn't so pushy. I found over medium the same way I found God. Family and friends and a boatload of mistakes. It's funny really. We either cling to the God of our parents, find our own, or go vegan. Good or not, so much of my understanding of God comes through other people. Here's to my path paved with mistakes.

When I Smoked

When I used to smoke in college, I'd drive to Salem at midnight and walk around downtown with my best friend, John, drinking black coffee and dragging off a cheap pack of cigarettes at the Coffee House Cafe. John was a rebel of sorts. I followed his lead. John went to Bible college and knew all of these really cool words about God that I'd never heard or even knew how to say. Bible college was still a few years out for me, so he'd explain mysterious and unpronounceable notions of the Holy that made almost no sense and definitely made God much more confusing than what I'd come to understand. John talked about *election* and the *hypostatic union* and *views of the atonement.* This was a new language for me. Smiling and nodding like I understood, I'd walk along with him under the streetlights of Salem to a park by the river. Later, I'd go back to college in Eugene and aerate his ideas for weeks on end, trying to come to grips with what he'd said. Over the years of trips to Salem with the coffee and cheap cigarettes, John cured my delusion of a God who was simple, easy, and understandable. After years of walking around Salem, I came to the conclusion that if God could be comprehended entirely by our rational, peabody minds and with the language we ourselves have constructed, then that was a rather puny God. But it also became clear that it was only *with words* that we could speak of God.

This created a problem. To talk about God inherently meant God's beauty was being butchered. But it was more important to talk about God poorly than not at all.

I once heard that G. K. Chesterton, the famed English writer and theologian, had said that all of the important things to do in life were worth doing poorly. For me, theology, talking about God, was one of them. It became a central notion of mine—that we don't talk about God because we fully understand God. *We talk about God because we want to search God out.*[1]

Because to *not* talk about God is worse than, if done in love, talking *inaccurately* about God. The big words about God that John taught me didn't always make sense; but then again, he concluded, maybe that was

---

1. There is a tiny little book by Pierre Bayard that talks about how to talk about books you have never read, aptly titled *How to Talk About Books You Haven't Read* (Bloomsbury, 2009). He kind of gets to the same point regarding books that I do here about God.

good. And that a God who required people to come up with words like *election*, or *hypostatic union*, or *atonement* must be a big God. It made sense to me as time went on, and I grew more and more comfortable with these long, multisyllabic notions. If God was big, so our words about him should be. Over time it became evident that these words held a certain authority for people. Especially if people didn't know them. It made them think I had a corner on God that they hadn't found. It made me feel special. For a while, these words came in handy, because I could use them and make other people feel like they didn't know as much about God as I did. Knowing these words gave a sort of power to their users. A secret power. As time went on it became even clearer, however, that these words didn't help normal everyday people, even though they were words I loved to use. Explaining the *hypostatic union* to a woman whose child just died was simply not right. Telling someone the importance of their view of *election* when they were addicted to drugs never seemed to help. Nor did discussing the *atonement* ever solve someone's pending divorce. These words are important, and are central to the Christian faith. But it's not about the words. It's about something deeper. Something I learned from the Swedish people.

IKEA gets theology.

IKEA, in large part, is a drug. People flock to it. One opened in Portland, and people flocked as if the Beatles were playing in the park or something. The whole experience really is incredible. From the minute you walk in you are toast. First, you have the meatballs. This is where they get you. Huge, saucy meatballs as you walk in that you can walk around with as you look at furniture and appliances. The selection is endless. You can't *not* get lost, and there are no windows to see if the light of day has ended. Frankly, you have to confess, the stuff the Swedish sell is cool. Look at the names of these products. *Vlectec. Frigginop. Yelter.* It's all in Swedish. It's impossible to know what they mean. You just know what they do. And people flock to this stuff. Like crazy. With meatballs in their hands and sauce on their cheeks. Because these products help people's lives and make sense and add beauty and value to their lives. *No one buys the stuff at IKEA because of the names of the products.* They buy them because they work. Ask anybody at IKEA, "Are you here for the *Frigginop?*" and they'll look at you and then start looking for security. The names are just the names. It's the thing behind the name we come for. It's not entirely clear what *atonement* exactly means, but I believe it because it works. It says, you can't earn God's love—*someone else made you "at one" with God.* Theology never claims that the ideas make complete sense; it just claims that they work. And that the things behind them are so incredibly beautiful and meaningful and give life to the user. Theology is only as good as it gets us to God. So too, Christianity is only as good as it gets us to Christ.

On How We Change But God Doesn't

John was my Lewis and Clark. He was really the first person to help me walk into the magical, new, wild and untouched world of theology.

But I've wiggled around in there for some time, wrestling and prodding, asking and seeking.

After years of being in the wilderness, I've unquestionably changed my mind many times about God and who God is. We all do this. Our theology is always in process, like one of those time-lapse videos of a blade of grass growing. For some time, I was taught to believe that if someone spoke in tongues, they were most likely possessed by a demon. Then someone I knew who wildly loved Jesus told me they did, so I backed off on that. Today I completely disagree with that old me. For a while, I was most certain that Jesus was coming back in glory at Y2K. Sitting up late in front of the television on December 31, 1999, I realized I was wrong. That didn't pan out so well. Then I also used to think that God chose who would go to heaven and personally chose who would go to hell. Almost certainly the reason I did this was because I could never believe in the idea that God would save me because of myself. It would totally have to be because he wanted to save me. No other reason. But after some time, it began to feel so ridiculously selfish to me that I thought God chose people for heaven *and I was pretty sure I was one of them.* Like a kid calling all his friends for a game of T-ball, picking both teams, and writing the rules for himself. Even if God chose who goes to heaven and who goes to hell, that was beyond my pay grade. I've changed. Here is what I am thinking after all this (so far). No matter how much I believe that God is always the same (which I do), *what I think about him hasn't remained the same.* The God I understood ten years ago is way different from the God I understand now. Does that mean God is changing? No. It means I'm a bonehead and need time to work out my thoughts. You are the same. Do astronomers understand exactly what a black hole is the minute they buy their first telescope as a kid?

Too much of our theology isn't about God. It's about us. Our own insecurities. If our thinking about God is constructed so that we can control God and make God more amiable to our comfortable lifestyles, it isn't good theology. Or a good God. Like a little windup monkey. As a kid, someone gave me a miniature windup monkey. It walked in circles, clanged its sharp silver cymbals, and then slowly came to a fading halt. I'd wind it up again. But nothing would change. It was so predictable. It was mechanical. It never surprised me. So I stopped winding it up and left it in the corner of my room. Many of us think of Jesus that way. He's where we say he is. He does what we say he does. He acts as we see fit. He's our monkey Jesus. And he's surprisingly boring. I call him our windup Jesus. There's another Jesus. He's wild, unpredictable, passionate, and rarely makes sense. Two millennia ago, he initiated a progressive and organic movement of people into an alternative lifestyle; they were willing to change and leave everything to follow him. For those who followed him, he was real and dynamic and dangerous. He hasn't changed. Even if our thinking about God has.

Some people say theology is a joke. Sam Harris and Richard Dawkins, two leading atheists, consider all theology to be a joke. They wrongly caricature Christians as thoughtless idiots who care nothing about truth. What is incredible is how similar Sam Harris and Richard Dawkins are to the man who helped Christianity change the world. Paul. Paul, a central figure in the development of Christianity from a group of first-generation disciples to a world-changing movement, had a tattered past. They still let him in. And let him pastor their churches. Paul was older when he followed Jesus. Maybe around forty years old. His final missionary journeys were when he was fifty or sixty years old. His story of conversion is rather confusing. In the book of Acts, we are told that after his experience with Jesus in the desert, he went even farther into the desert for three years in the land of Arabia.[2] It must have been an odd experience for him, because he doesn't write about his Arabia experience anywhere else in any of his letters. After some time in the desert with his new friend Jesus, Paul returns in zeal to go and preach the message of Christ. At first, the Christian communities were rather uncomfortable with Paul because his previous life was all about killing Christians. But after some time, they received him as an apostle. The story of Paul in the early church should mean something today.

The greatest leaders in Christianity are converted heretics.

There is room and always will be room in the Christian movement for those who used to be wrong. It's scary though. Imagine if your new pastor were Sam Harris after he realized he was wrong.

Knowing

When we say we *know* something, we almost always mean we know a fact about it. This is surprisingly unbiblical. Sure, there is a sense of *knowing about* something in the Bible. In the New Testament, the word *ginōskō*, "to know," carries with it the sense that we have cognitive and rational understanding of something. This is head-knowing.

But those who wrote the Old Testament often used another word

---

2. Galatians 1:11–24, esp. vv. 17–18.

for knowing. *Yada*. *Yada* was a kind of *knowing* that was much more expansive in its concept. This kind of knowing is much more intimate. Much more relational. Much more touchable. *Yada*, as with so many other Hebrew words, has two meanings. First, it means "to know." Then, and closely related, it means "to have sex with." For Hebrews, to know something is to *know* something. This is why, in the story of Mary and Joseph when he finds out about her pregnancy before their marriage, the Bible says that before they were married he didn't *know* her. This is like the *yada* know. Too often I know God in the *ginōskō* sense. We need more *yada*. The beauty of life is knowing God intimately. To live with God and be known by God and become like God in all that we do. In Christianity, we believe this is only possible when we are in relationship with God. In this relationship, where both are vulnerable with one another, life takes place. But how do we enter this relationship? How do we find intimacy with God?

Theology is a lot like foreplay; it's the stuff we do to get to the *real* thing. That's why I call theology foreplay. It should always lead to something yet is never the point in itself. That might sound crude, but I think it's true. When we read good theology, it forces us to rethink everything. Rehash assumptions. Challenge answers. All for the sake and search for reality. If it doesn't take us to the cross or the tomb, it takes us nowhere. And it takes us a long time to come to good conclusions about God. Any other kind of theology is McDoctrine. And it isn't good. In the 1940s, Swiss-German theologian Karl Barth wrote a thirteen-volume set of theology called *Church Dogmatics*. It is ridiculous and long. Barth (pronounced "bart") spent the last thirty years of his life writing it, never actually finishing it. Near the end of his life, someone asked Barth to sum up, for the normal reader, his entire theology in the thirteen volumes.

After being asked, Barth said that his entire theology said "Jesus loves me this I know, for the Bible tells me so."

Through all the complexity and craziness of his theology, he arrived at the conclusion that Jesus loved him. These are the kinds of people I want to be like. People like Augustine, Karl Barth, John Piper, Donald Bloesch, Athanasius, Martin Luther—they wake up my soul. A friend told me the key to reading good theology is to skip the first aisle at the Christian bookstore. I kind of agree. I've made a tradition out of reading both the *living* and the *dead*. Because sometimes the sexiest theology of our day is not the thing we should be thinking of. Sometimes the dead get at truth more than the living. C. S. Lewis said he would read three old books for every new one. I read three dead people for every one living. I think that reading good theology is central to being a follower of Jesus. It is the way we challenge our frail and imperfect thoughts about God. But *reading* theology is only half of the deal. To read it and not do it is the same as walking up to the table of communion and staring at it. But that isn't what communion is for. It is for eating. So is theology. To do it right is to eat good theology and live it. Do it. Practice it.

Wrestling with God

God doesn't have a theology. He has himself. His theology is his mirror. It is very personal. If he wants to know more about himself, he talks to himself. It's a very personal affair. In the Old Testament, whenever God speaks to a prophet about himself, the Scripture will say, "And the word of the Lord came to so and so." It came to Jonah. It came to Isaiah. It came to Elijah. The word of the Lord came to the prophet. What is odd is that in the entire life of Jesus, the Scripture never says, "And the word of the Lord came to Jesus." It didn't need to. When you are the Word, you don't need a word. Had it said, "And the word of the Lord came to Jesus," it might as well have said, "And Jesus talked to himself." We do have a theology. But because most of us are confused about how pathetic we are, we do the same thing God does. When we want to know our theology, so often we look in the mirror. And it becomes a very personal affair. To me, so much of our (and my) theology looks like us. I have found that the problem with the Bible is, it doesn't fit into my theology.

Everything we do as human beings proclaims the theology that we nurture and care for in our heart. When we hate our neighbor for being of a certain religion or political party, it proclaims to the world what we think about God. Or when we forgive someone for hurting us, we pronounce to the world something about what we believe about God. Our way of life is God's microphone. Our life preaches. Everything we do. When we accept this, we realize that there is ultimately no way to actually escape the necessity of theology in our lives. Theology is something we do, not just something we believe. The same is true for church. At our community gatherings on Sunday, we begin every gathering with a communal meal and end every gathering by taking the Eucharist—the body and blood of Christ. Nothing has been more important for us. How we do the Lord's Supper screams what we think about God. When we have the children in our church serve the adults the bread and juice, *it says something about God*. When we allow both men and women to serve communion, *it says something about God*. When we allow sinners to come to the table, *it says something about God*. If you don't come to the table as broken as the bread and as dark as the wine, then you don't deserve to partake. When any follower of Christ is invited to the table, even if they go to a different church, *it says something about God*. Communion, the mysterious proclamation of Christ's love, is incredible. At the body and blood of Christ in the bread and wine, we are confronted with a God big enough to save us from our sins and tiny enough to get stuck between your teeth.

But we all learn about hiding from scary stuff from a young age. Secretly, having a stepdad wasn't always peaches and cream. I remember sitting across the table from him and thinking, *You actually think you are my dad? Stop fooling yourself. You're not, so stop calling me "Son" and "Skipper." I'm from another.* With grace, I never actually said those words out loud, but boy do I remember them. Mike, my stepfather, was a very good second father to me. Sometimes when he would come home after a long day at work, he would help my mom make dinner, do the dishes, and help in the yard. Sometimes he would wrestle with me and my stepbrother. This was tricky. I didn't want him to actually think I enjoyed this wrestling tomfoolery. If it was to work right, I would get to wrestle with him but in the end not give him the satisfaction of knowing I actually had a good time. And sometimes it would work; we would wrestle for like ten minutes; then I would fake a broken arm so he felt bad. That way I had fun and he felt like an idiot. But there were other times. These were when we would wrestle for forty-five minutes straight, tossing and turning, sweating and spitting, roughing it up, and I couldn't help but laugh and giggle like a boy on bubbles. And after the dust had settled, he would sit there, and I would sit there, and we would laugh.

If I was in a bind, there was a couch I would sometimes hide behind to get away from him. But because he is six foot five, he could just crawl over it. There was no use in hiding, because he could just go over it. All the more I realize now that he was opening the joy of fatherhood that seemed lost, and I opened the joy of sonhood surely lost. Because, like a good dad, he would sometimes let me win. If I wrestled God, I'm sure I'd win. He seems like that kind of God to me. Not weak or powerless per se; just the kind of God I could take down. Especially if it is Jesus we are talking about. I mean, the whole temple thing was cool, flipping tables and all, but he seems rather weak for a God, rather simple, rather "wrestle-able." He is the kind of God that might let you win, and when you thought it all was over, he'd rise again on the third day, just to prove to us he was God. But he'd sometimes let us win. Like Jacob did.[3] Yet I'm sure it'd hurt. Hiding behind a chair never worked. Mike was too big. Hiding behind lies never works. God is too big. We hide behind things because we don't want to face reality. Sometimes, and rightly so,

---

3. Genesis 32:22–32.

we get scared to open ourselves up to being wrong. It means we have to let the old us die. But if we are unwilling to open ourselves up to a greater understanding of truth, we are not truth seekers. Put it another way. To hide behind a lie in Jesus' name rejects the Jesus who is the way, the truth, and the life.[4] Wherever that truth may be. Even if it isn't in our own denomination.

Of the twenty-two thousand denominations in the world, you probably *aren't* in the right one.

They're all wrong. Jesus is right. Donald Bloesch says, "True orthodoxy is a willingness to make oneself vulnerable for the sake of the gospel."[5] That is, our gospel forces us to admit that we are wrong and need correction. Otherwise we are following a false gospel. That means there always has to be room in our theology *of* Jesus *for* Jesus. We must make room in our understanding of God for God to be God. Otherwise we are not accepting God for who God is. The rabbis teach that even God is wrestling with the Bible. If you want God to accept you for who you are, you need to accept him for who he is.

Someone else once said that the job of the theologian isn't to stand at heaven's door and check passports.[6] That's God's job description. Never ours. We are all theologians. And we must understand what our role is.

And also what it's not.

---

4. John 14:6.
5. Donald G. Bloesch, *A Theology of Word and Spirit: Authority and Method in Theology*, Christian Foundations 1 (Downers Grove, IL: InterVarsity Press, 1992), 24.
6. Amos Yong, *Beyond the Impasse: Toward a Pneumatological Theology of Religions* (Grand Rapids: Baker Academic, 2002), 50.

CHAPTER ELEVEN

Curtain: Messy Life

Some people believe in retirement. I won't be sure till I get there, but I'm relatively sure I'm never going to retire. The idea isn't overwhelmingly inspiring. Work your whole life to golf. It's unconvincing. Not that retirement is wrong. It's just for other people. Not to mention the only notion in the Bible that vaguely resembles retirement as we know it, is called death.[1] I may not retire. But I will end. And so will everyone else. Everyone moves from present tense to past tense.

---

1. Numbers 8:23–26 does cap active service in setting up the tent of meeting and performing their duties at forty-nine, but the fifty-something Levites were still to continue ministering to their younger fellow Levites by keeping guard (aka "active retirement").

The Beginning and the End

I rarely like things to end. I'm very nostalgic in that way. The day after graduating from high school, I drove my little red truck down to the school and walked around the grounds for a couple of hours, super sad that it was all over. Which is funny. Because high school wasn't really that great. *Why would I mourn that?* But we all do that, to some degree. We all walk around something and mope about something that ended which wasn't that great. But our minds remember it as this incurable thing. It's interesting, isn't it, that the old days are always good and the todays are always darker? We enshrine the past in glory and whine about today as if it's horrible.

My parents watch the five o'clock news, like I used to, and are super convinced the world is on its way to hell. *They should stop watching it, I tell them.* When they tell me this, I put it back on them and ask if the days when they were kids weren't dark. They had to hide under desks during bomb drills. They admitted their days were dark. But at least they were done. The problem isn't that these days are still dark; it's that they just aren't done. We humans do that. We conjure up an endless sense of negative inevitability, that something is always about to happen. Something bad. All the time. Around every corner. The sky is always minutes from falling. After we've lived for some time, we discover that God's ways are unique. He runs his ship different than others do. He probably knows what he's doing. I think that God is all-knowing. That means a lot of things. It also doesn't mean a lot of things. But, to me, it does mean that he knows if this book will sell, yet he won't tell me ahead of time when I want to know. Someone still needs to write it. If God is all-knowing, it sometimes feels like he rubs it in our face. But he isn't. Maybe it's good that God doesn't tell us everything. We humans find it nearly impossible to do what we're supposed to do *today* let alone worry about next week. Frankly, and this is just my gut, if God actually did tell us what our life would be like in a month, we'd all need adult Depends.

God's Will

God's will is real. It's how we understand it that is messed up. Some people sit up till dusk worrying about everything, thinking if they don't do his will perfectly, they're toast. Jesus redeems this. He spends almost no time during his life asking what God's will is. He just does it. Sure, he had a moment or two where it is in question, like when he was in the garden of Gethsemane and asked the Father, if he could, to take the cross away from him. But Jesus never talks about wondering what God's will for his life is. Maybe this was because worrying about what God's will is, keeps you from *doing* God's will.

There was this boss that I had at a church once who was really hard to work for. He hired me to be a college pastor, and then I rarely heard from him again. No direction. No vision. No nothing. Setting up a meeting with him, I told him I was frustrated that he wasn't telling me what to do. So I asked him, "What do you want me to do?" He smiled, and then said, "Go 'til I say no." Jesus' yes is often hidden in his silence. Meaning, if God doesn't want me to do something, it is on him to communicate that. Some of the greatest decisions in your life will happen when you don't hear a yes. It will happen when God doesn't say no. If God wants you to hear a no, he's good at that. And if you aren't hearing a no, God's doing a bad job of communicating. And God seems to be good at communicating.

God has a will. But it's mysterious. The mysteriousness of God's will is a lot like Lewis and Clark making a map. It's *discovered along the way.* So many of the decisions we made in the past are often ways to get out of our own personal responsibility. God told me to do this. God told me to do that. We don't know if we found the way until after we've made it home. I believe God can use our mistakes more than our inactions. Sometimes it seems like we think God is this referee walking around wanting to call technical fouls on everyone for making mistakes. Salvation in Jesus says God turns that stuff into good. Christianity has done a marvelous job of turning the idea of redemption and salvation into this far-off thing. That salvation is the far and far. We have a challenging duty in redeeming redemption for not only heaven, but heaven coming to earth.[2] The Jews never had any idea of heaven as we have it in their theology.

Curtain

There is hope everywhere. In all of creation. Even in Shakespeare. I'm a fan of theatre geeks. I'm one of them. Shakespeare is a blast. You sound smart when you say you read it for fun. You sound like a genius when you can quote it. I have a friend who is British. He can say the dumbest stuff in the world, but when he does it in a British accent, he sounds so freaking smart. Since my British accent was horrible, I did the next best thing. High school drama. High school gave me the chance to be in a Shakespeare play. The only one I was in was called *As You Like It*. Apparently my audition went really, really well. So well that Mrs. Baker assigned me to the role of "Forest Lord #1." You know you're relatively useless to the plot of the story when your character's name has the word "Forest" in it. I remember reading the thing for the first time. It made no sense. At all. I didn't know if my character was a man, a woman, a jolly ole cow. Really. It made no sense. I'm still not sure what the play was about to this day. Now, in the midst of my confusion I did have two plot-thickening lines. I still remember one of the two. *"Indeed, my lord, / The melancholy Jacque grieves at that, / And, in that kind, swears you do more usurp / That doth your brother that hath banish'd you."* Riveting. And even at that, I forgot it one of the performances. Because it was a hard play to act and understand, we would practice all the time.

To practice for this brilliant masterpiece that none of us understood, we'd play this game called Zap, where we'd stand in a circle and do

---

2. This is a major theme in a very helpful book by Scot McKnight, *Embracing Grace: A Gospel for All of Us* (Paraclete, 2005), esp. 79–82.

these little made-up scenes to improve our acting skills. It's called improvisational acting. Aka—"bad" acting. Two people would improvise a scene and when someone else mustered up the strength or wanted to, they'd say, "Zap," tap someone out, and start a new scene where the last scene left off. It was always interesting. We tried to be creative, but it always ended up being about some bank robbery, or a heart attack, or hunting, or something stupid like that. And there was always that one guy who took it way too seriously and would "zap" himself into a scene and try to fit into whatever position everyone was in, and start giving the Gettysburg Address or something. He'd always work it out somehow, finding some way for Abraham Lincoln to actually give CPR while delivering one of the greatest speeches in American history. And when we were done, and we really needed a new start, someone would say, "Curtain." If the scene got so dumb and so confusing and so stupid that we needed to start over, someone would end the scene and scream out "Curtain!" I said it a lot. But then you knew it was all done. "Curtain." Then it was all over. Finally. Over. New game.

Shakespeare wrote his plays in two genres: comedies and tragedies. A genre is a kind of literature that helps us understand its overall purpose. It's a category that allows us to decide how something is to be read. The genre, which is always clear after you read the whole thing, deeply affects the way you read it in entirety. This is important for reading the Bible. I teach the Bible at a seminary, and genre changes massively the way we live our life and form our theology. Determining the genre is the reason people don't cut out their eyes when they watch a bad movie and why we let ourselves wear poly blends. Jesus said, "If your right eye causes you to sin, gouge it out and throw it away."[3] Thankfully, we have interpreted that relatively scary piece of literature as what we call hyperbole. Overstatement. The book of Deuteronomy says it is

---

3. Matthew 5:29.

not lawful for someone to wear anything with more than one kind of material woven into the fabric. Again, most interpret that to be part of what is called "purity" codes, which are intended to give living in the woods and learning how to stay clean, a good name.[4]

Point is: genre changes everything.

It shapes everything. The way we live our lives is changed by genre. In Shakespeare, there's a huge difference between comedies and tragedies. All comedies, like *As You Like It*, have one thing in common, and all tragedies have one thing in common. A comedy ends with a wedding, and a tragedy ends with a death (usually a suicide). Now catch this: ever consider that the only thing that makes a genre what it is in Shakespeare's plays is what happens at the end? And the genre makes all the difference. But the end makes the genre. *Remember, the genre changes everything.* Let me prove it to you. Next time you watch a movie or play you have already seen, pay attention to what you know: *when you know how it ends, it changes how you watch the middle, doesn't it?* Ever watched a movie you've already seen and in your head you're trying to tell the character what to do because you know the monster is hiding in *that closet*? When you know the end, you know the best for everyone in the story, don't you? For someone who knows the genre, it changes the way they watch the middle. And I'm sure, with Shakespeare's plays, people would find out what genre it was. Their friend, who would go and see the play first, would then come back and tell them how it ends. Then when that person would go see it, they would be able to endure the middle because they know how the whole thing finishes up. They'd come home and say to their neighbor, who hasn't seen it yet, "Well the middle's as boring as all get out, but you'll make it through. The end rocks."

If you knew it was a comedy, and it ended with a huge wedding, it wouldn't matter how sad or depressing or hopeless the middle was; *you*

---

4. Deuteronomic code teaches this in the Old Testament.

knew the whole thing ended with a party. And if you know it's a tragedy, and it ended with death, it wouldn't matter how funny, or happy, or likeable the middle got; *you still knew it ended in death.*

I was thinking about that, and for the first time I got something. In all my semipathetic, confused, and half-baked quasi understanding of God, the world, the Bible, and everything else in between, that's the only way in my vocabulary to articulate as best I know how what I think Jesus is for humanity. *Jesus changes the genre of his followers from a tragedy to a comedy.* The good news is, we have a new end.

But the mess is, we're still in the middle.

BIBLIOGRAPHY

Amsberry, John. *More of You Through Prayer.*
Bloomington, IN: AuthorHouse, 2009.

Anderson, David A. *Gracism: The Art of Inclusion.*
Downers Grove, IL: InterVarsity Press, 2007.

Bainton, Roland H. *Here I Stand: A Life of Martin
Luther.* New York: Abingdon-Cokesbury,
1950.

Barth, Karl. *The Holy Spirit and the Christian Life:
The Theological Basis of Ethics.* Translated by
R. Birch Hoyle. 1938. Louisville: Westminster/
John Knox Press, 1993.

Bartholomew, Craig G., and Michael W. Goheen.
*The Drama of Scripture: Finding Our Place in the
Biblical Story.* Grand Rapids: Baker Academic,
2004.

Bayard, Pierre. *How to Talk About Books You Haven't
Read.* 2008. Translated by Jeffrey Mehlman.
New York: Bloomsbury, 2009.

Baylis, Albert H. *From Creation to the Cross:
Understanding the First Half of the Bible.* Grand
Rapids: Zondervan, 1996.

Bloesch, Donald G. *A Theology of Word and Spirit:
Authority and Method in Theology.* Christian
Foundations 1. Downers Grove, IL: InterVarsity
Press, 1992.

————. *Holy Scripture: Revelation, Inspiration and Interpretation*, Christian Foundations 2. Downers Grove, IL: InterVarsity Press, 1994.

Bonhoeffer, Dietrich. *Christology*. 1963. Translated by John Bowden. New York: Harper & Row, 1966.

Brown, Peter. *Augustine of Hippo: A Biography*. 1967. New ed. Berkeley: University of California Press, 2000.

Brown, William P. *The Ethos of the Cosmos: The Genesis of Moral Imagination in the Bible*. Grand Rapids: Eerdmans, 1999.

Cadbury, Henry J. *The Peril of Modernizing Jesus*. Lowell Institute Lectures, 1937. London: SPCK, 1962..

Carson, D. A., ed., with Mark Ashton, R. Kent Hughes, and Timothy J. Keller. *Worship by the Book*. Grand Rapids: Zondervan, 2002.

Clines, David J. A. *Job 1–20*. Word Biblical Commentary. Dallas, TX: Word, 1989.

Coupland, Douglas. *Marshall McLuhan: You Know Nothing of My Work!* New York: Atlas & Co., 2010.

Cummings, Charles. *Eco-Spirituality: Toward a Reverent Life*. Mahwah, NJ: Paulist Press, 1991.

Dawn, Marva J. *Reaching Out Without Dumbing Down: A Theology of Worship for the Turn-of-the-Century Culture*. Grand Rapids: Eerdmans, 1995.

————. *A Royal Waste of Time: The Splendor of Worshiping God and Being Church for the World*. Grand Rapids: Eerdmans, 1999.

Gelpi, Donald L. *The Divine Mother: A Trinitarian Theology of the Holy Spirit*. Lanham, MD: University Press of America, 1984.

Gunton, Colin E. *The One, the Three, and the Many: God, Creation, and the Culture of Modernity*. Cambridge: Cambridge University Press, 1993.

Halter, Hugh, and Matt Smay. *The Tangible Community: Creating Incarnational Community*. San Francisco: Jossey-Bass, 2008.

Hauerwas, Stanley. *A Community of Character: Toward a Constructive*

Christian Social Ethic. Notre Dame, IN: University of Notre Dame Press, 1981.

Heschel, Abraham Joshua. *I Asked for Wonder: A Spiritual Anthology*. Edited by Samuel H. Dresner. New York: Crossroad, 1983.

Lynch, Thomas. *Bodies in Motion and at Rest: On Metaphor and Morality*. New York: W. W. Norton & Co., 2000.

McKnight, Scot. *The Blue Parakeet: Rethinking How You Read the Bible*. Grand Rapids: Zondervan, 2008.

———. *Embracing Grace: A Gospel for All of Us* (Brewster, MA: Paraclete, 2005).

Peterson, Eugene H. *Five Smooth Stones for Pastoral Work*. 1980. Grand Rapids: Eerdmans, 1992.

Schmidt, Thomas E. *Straight and Narrow? Compassion and Clarity in the Homosexuality Debate*. Downers Grove, IL: InterVarsity Press, 1995.

Smith, Jonathan Z. *Map Is Not Territory: Studies in the History of Religion*. 1978. Chicago: University of Chicago Press, 1993.

Spoto, Donald. *The Reluctant Saint: The Life of Francis of Assisi*. New York: Viking Compass, 2002.

Steinsaltz, Adin. *Biblical Images*. 1984. Enl. ed. Translated by Yehuda Hanegbi and Yehudit Keshet. Northvale, NJ: Jason Aronson, 1994.

Sweet, Leonard. *Nudge: Awakening Each Other to the God Who's Already There*. Colorado Springs: David C. Cook, 2010.

———. *The Three Hardest Words in the World to Get Right*. Colorado Springs: Waterbrook, 2006.

White, Mel. *Stranger at the Gate: To Be Gay and Christian in America*. 1994. New York: Penguin, 1995.

Yong, Amos. *Beyond the Impasse: Toward a Pneumatological Theology of Religions*. Grand Rapids: Baker Academic, 2002.

Žižek, Slavoj. *The Parallax View*. Short Circuits. Cambridge, MA: MIT Press, 2006.

ABOUT THE AUTHOR

A.J. Swoboda (PhD, Theology—University of Birmingham, UK) is a professor of theology, biblical studies, and Christian history at George Fox Evangelical Seminary in Portland, Oregon. He also teaches at LIFE Pacific College, Canby Bible College, Eternity Bible College, the Episcopal Academy of Formation, and Concordia University. A.J. and his wife, Quinn, started and serve the *Theophilus* church community in the Hawthorne District of Portland, Oregon (www.theophiluschurch .com). Prior to this, A.J. served as a campus pastor at the University of Oregon. His creative doctoral research explored the never-ending relationship between the Holy Spirit and ecology in the Pentecostal and Charismatic traditions. Besides his doctoral thesis, *Tongues and Trees: Towards a Green Pentecostal Pneumatology*, *Messy* is his first book. For fun, A.J. plays with his son, Elliot, writes, wails on guitars, runs (mostly treadmills), plays Settlers, reads, and has a predisposition toward movies with Kevin Spacey in them. His website and blog are found at www.ajswoboda.com and you can follow him on Twitter @mrajswoboda.